"YOU COULDN'T

ACKNOWLEDGEMENTS

The authors would like to thank the following for their assistance:

Manx National Heritage Library Staff

Robert Hendry

Flora Callow

The Sector Marshals

Keith Trubshaw

Dick Hawes

George Gelling

Paul Kniveton

The Cringle Family

Doreeen Douglas

Adrian Cowin

Andrew Pennington

Crossleys, the Accountants

Leslie Vondy, J.P.

Victor Kneale, C.B.E., J.P.

Muriel

Manning Printing Limited

... and countless others

Graphics by K. Ennett
© Peter Beighton and Andrew Douglas 1993
ISBN 1 898363 00 5
Printed and Published by Mannin Printing Limited

FOREWORD

YOU COULDN'T DO IT NOW!

Just suppose for a minute that for some reason there had never been any road racing on the Isle of Man. Just suppose that it's the mid 1990's and the A.C.U. decide to approach the authorities in the Island with a view to holding races on closed roads . . .

They would be asking for –
- An Act of Parliament to close the roads, including many which run right past people's houses so they can't get in or out during practices and races.
- A commitment to keeping the course in first class order.
- The co-operation of an entire police force.
- 1,200 volunteers from on and off the Island to act as marshals, first-aiders, time-keepers, commentators and host of other things.
- A tidy amount of Government funding.
- Fund raisers to guarantee enough money for a helicopter.

. . . and so on.

You couldn't do it now!

Why not? Because the TT Races on the Isle of Man were born and grew up with the car and bike. What you see these days is the mature version; a rounded, experienced event.

Together with my co-authors, I will transport you back to the beginning, to the birth pangs and prangs of the TT. Edwardian dare-devils racing tons of metal round farmers' tracks with men at the ready to let a train pass over a level crossing if there was no bike in sight! I'll take you through the childhood of the TT when it sometimes had its gears boxed but somehow managed to grow and prosper. Finally I'll take you round this famous course, naming and pointing out the best and the unusual vantage spots.

I hope you will get as much enjoyment reading the book as I have in helping to write it. I just wanted TT fans everywhere to get more out of the world's greatest road races.

Cheers.

Steve.

THE ISLE OF MAN – ITS LOCATION, HISTORY AND CULTURE

Many of the readers will be familiar with the Isle of Man already, but for the first time visitor and we suspect the regular TT devotee, many of the facts about the Island are submerged beneath the welter of race information and folklore thrust at them on arrival on the shores of Ellan Vannin.

Set in the Irish Sea, midway between the coasts of England, Ireland, Scotland and Wales, the Island measures at its extremities 33 miles (52kms) by 13 miles (22kms) and has a land mass area of some 227 square miles (572 sq.kms).

Although it is a comparatively small island it offers a wide variety of scenery covering virtually every type found elsewhere in the British Isles. Encompassed within over 100 miles (160km) of coastline there is a central range of mountains and hills lying in a North Easterly/South Westerly direction, with well defined valleys leading down to rocky cliffs and sheltered bays. This contrasts with the flat Northern plain with its long sandy beaches.

In recent years the Island has experienced a growth in its resident population to the present level of some 70,000. This gives a density level of just 308 people per square mile (122 per sq.kms) so there is plenty of room in which to move around.

The major centre of population is based in Douglas, the Island's capital, with approximately 22,000 inhabitants, with a further 28,000 living in seven other main towns and villages.

The Isle of Man has an equable climate lacking in extremes, escaping the harsh variations experienced in the rest of the British Isles by virtue of its location and the warming influence of the Gulf Stream which runs around the shoreline. Prevailing winds blow from the South West giving varying degrees of shelter and exposure island wise, due to the rugged nature of the topography. In summer, the months of April, May and June are usually the driest whilst May, June and July are the sunniest. July and August are the warmest months with an average daily maximum temperature around 17.4°C (63°F). Rarely in the year does the temperature fall below zero.

Rich in history, the Isle of Man can look back on a tapestry of events from the introduction of farming in the fourth millennium BC, the Manx Iron Age from 500 BC to 500 AD, the Celtic traditions, through to Christianity and Viking rule. In more recent times, Sovereignty passed frequently between Scotland and England, with occasional incursions from Ireland to be dealt with.

By the eighteenth century, it had become a major centre for the smuggling trade and to put a stop to this, the British Government stepped up its interest in the Isle of Man, by purchasing the entire Island for just £70,000.

Events as described above have left the Island with a unique culture and distinctive heritage of its own, which is carefully safeguarded to this day.

Welcome to our Island, we hope you enjoy it as much as we enjoy living here.

CONTENTS

	Foreword	3
	The Isle of Man – Its Location, History and Culture	4
	Introduction	7
Chapter 1	Why Did It Start?	9
Chapter 2	The Early Courses and Races	13
Chapter 3	The Way Forward	23
Chapter 4	1907 And All That	33
Chapter 5	The Four-Inch Course	45
Chapter 6	The Mountain Circuit	53
Chapter 7	Hislop: His Lap	59
	Key	61
	Index	62
	Maps	65

"You Couldn't Do It Now!"

is dedicated to

the people

who did.

INTRODUCTION

Paris 1897 . . . It's hard to imagine that the first seeds of the Isle of Man Tourist Trophy Motorcycle Races were about to be sown.

An ocean away from Europe, Gordon Bennett Snr. the proprietor of the New York Herald, and part owner of the Bennett-Mackay Trans-Atlantic telephone cable, sent his son James Gordon Bennett to Paris to set up the continental edition of the family newspaper. Gordon Bennett quickly took to European lifestyle. He embraced amongst his many interests a fascination, a keen and passionate love affair with the automobile. This interest was to lead him to becoming a founder member of the French Automobile Club and in turn the proposer, in 1900, of the Gordon Bennett Cup, which eventually led to the foundation of the T.T Races ... but more of that later.

In the early years of the century, British manufacturing was going through a crisis. After the glorious Victorian era, a mood of despondency gripped the nation; lack of direction and loss of confidence were the norm. The fledgling automobile industry was struggling with prejudices and vested interests, all doing their best to crush the growing number of automobile manufacturers.

To men of vision working their way out of this period of stagnation was a priority. Obviously the restrictions placed on the automobile by the regressive British Government had to be overcome. The ridiculous speed limit of 14 miles per hour and the effective ban on racing had to be removed. Although the speed limit was raised ever higher over the years, the official attitude towards racing on public roads has never really changed. The flame of British inventiveness, whilst at times almost extinguished, is fortunately never quite allowed to die out.

Across the Channel, the Continentals were producing machines that even in the early 1900's were capable of moving at speeds of one mile a minute. These exciting achievements were made possible because racing was permissible on public roads in countries such as France, Belgium, Germany and Austria.

Back home the search for a suitable venue was on. It was never going to be easy. Not only did the terrain have to suit, but there had to be political will and public support. Mixed into this complex equation came the Isle of Man; its Governor, Lord Raglan; the Island's Parliament, Tynwald; and the Secretary of the Automobile Club of Great Britain and Ireland, Julian Orde.

Success is only achieved by good planning, hard work and total commitment. Fortunately for motor sport, the Island had all of these virtues in plentiful supply. The search was over. Since their inception the Tourist Trophy Races have been in the vanguard of motorcycle development and indeed it would not be too boastful a claim to make that the Isle of Man is the is the true birthplace of British motorsport.

"You couldn't do it now!" is not intended to be a definitive history of the TT. It is a tribute to the riders and the legions of people across the decades who have donated their skills, given of their time and devoted their holidays, most without monetary reward, to ensuring the TT remains the world's greatest road racing series.

WHY DID IT START? (1)

As the automobile gained in popularity, mankind's inquisitive mind turned to the future use of wheeled transport. Quite naturally, the spirit of competition soon surfaced.

Over in Paris, Gordon Bennett became heavily involved in arguing the pros and cons of American automobiles against their European rivals. Such was his enthusiasm that in 1900 he put up a trophy for competition between nations to decide who had the best motorised vehicle.

Rules were quickly compiled and covered such basics as: "The race was to be over a distance of 342 miles minimum (550 kilometres); by teams of three cars that were to weigh not more than one tonne (1000kg) each; and which had been wholly constructed in an entrant's own country; with the drivers being members of their own national club."

On the 14 June 1900, the first Gordon Bennett race took place over a 352 mile course between Paris and Lyon. Challenges to the French came from Germany and Belgium. The actual Race turned out to be quite a poorly organised affair with the few competitors having difficulty finding their way to Lyon, or indeed even in finishing.

After the experiences of 1900 the French Automobile Club decided that it would be best to run the 1901 cup contest in conjunction with the annual Paris to Bordeaux race, over a slightly reduced distance of 350 miles. This was the year of only one foreign entry, England's Mr S.F. Edge driving a 50 h.p. Napier, but alas he suffered so badly with his English tyres that rather than give up he fitted French tyres which earned him disqualification.

Such was the crushing superiority of the French manufacturers that there seemed little point in entering British automobiles in open competition against them. A lack of testing facilities meant that British component parts were largely unproven. Early retirement was the norm for those few British independents prepared to take the battle into the opposition camp.

Interest in competing in the race did however surface in England in 1902.

We won!

Competitors raced between Paris and Innsbruck, a distance of some 351.5 miles and found the French supremacy under some threat. The French entered three vehicles; a Panhard, a Mors and a Girardot but the latter two retired early in the Race. The Panhard driven by Chevalier Rene de Knyff had entered Austria with what appeared to be an unassailable lead but hard driving on the Austrian roads broke his differential and his heart. England's Edge driving the much improved Napier was the only driver to complete the course, to bring the Trophy home to Britain.

As it had been decided that the winning nation would host the following year's event, there was at first some consternation that Great Britain would be unable to fulfil its obligation. The racing of automobiles on public roads was prohibited by an Act of Parliament. This was after all a period in the country's history when the nation's spirit of adventure was all but submerged. The cloak of officialdom lay heavily across the land.

However, it was noted that the formal title of the club was the Automobile Club of Great Britain and Ireland. The Irish Parliament was quick to seize the opportunity of hosting the Race whilst the English sat with their heads buried in their gaskets. With a determination seldom seen in Irish politics, an Act was swiftly passed which not only brought racing on public roads to the Emerald Isle but also secured the immediate future of the series.

Athy in County Kildare, some 40 miles south west of Dublin, seemed to be the right, sparsely populated location. Racing a distance of 327.5 miles over several laps of a figure of eight circuit, the defending champion Edge received a warm welcome from the Irish spectators but eight punctures cost him two and a half hours and he was last by a long way. The 1903 winner was the German driver Jenatzy, bringing the 1904 Race to the Bad Homburg circuit in the Taunus mountains of Germany.

Interest in the Race was now increasing amongst the leaders of the infant British automobile fraternity, although it seems that the political leaders of the day had still not yet grasped the real value of motorised wheeled transport. It was almost as if the authorities of the day were waiting to be dragged kicking and screaming into the twentieth century.

Fortunately even in the darkest of times in a country's development, there are always men of vision to be found. Perhaps now it was time for the privateers to hand over the responsibility for carrying the flag to the manufacturers. National pride in the British automobile was spreading but there remained a good deal of catching up to be done if British vehicles were to be amongst the leaders. Facilities were urgently required to aid the promotion of the all British racing machine. What was needed was an open road circuit covering a selection of road conditions with a choice of gradients designed to test men and machines to the limits of their physical and mechanical capabilities.

Obviously racing on the highways and by-ways of Britain was impossible, forbidden by Act of Parliament and by the introduction in 1903 of a 20 m.p.h. speed restriction. So how was national pride and the future development of the automobile to survive, against the well established practices already in existence in Europe and America? The answer lay with the Secretary of the Automobile Club of Great Britain and Ireland, Julian, later to be Sir Julian Orde. He set off in February 1904 for the Isle of Man because he had a fairly shrewd idea that the Manx authorities might very well adopt a more conciliatory attitude to the racing of automobiles on public roads.

He was right of course, but he did have at least one ace up his sleeve. The Governor of the Isle of Man at the time was His Excellency The Right Honourable George Fitzroy Henry, The Baron Raglan . . . Julian's cousin.

What Orde found in the Isle of Man in the spring of 1904, was an enthusiasm for racing that permeated through all stratas of Island life, both branches of Tynwald (the Manx Parliament), from public officials and from the ordinary man and woman in the streets of Ellan Vannin. All wanted to offer the British automobile industry a home, a chance to hold the eliminating trials for the Gordon Bennett International Races under near perfect conditions.

There was no killjoy spirit abroad in this part of the British Islands. With a young and developing tourist industry, a new opportunity was eagerly seized.

Lord Raglan listened carefully to the propositions put before him and considered the situation because, after all, here was an island that less than two hundred years before had only just begun to see the introduction of any form of wheeled transport; everything prior to that date had been moved around by pack horse or, on high ground, by sledge. Were the Manx people ready to have their tranquil way of life shattered by roaring, snorting metal monsters, roaming at will around the towns, villages and countryside? The Governor worried less than anybody because he had discovered what many visitors to the Isle of Man have learned over the centuries – that the Manx are adaptable and are able to blend the essence of the past with the rich veins of the future.

A month after Orde's visit to his cousin, Tynwald sat on the 15th. March 1904, to be presented with a Bill entitled The Highways (Light Locomotive) Act 1904, designed to permit the racing of automobiles on the public roads of the Isle of Man during one day and not exceeding three days in the year. Tynwald decreed that there was to be no racing on Sundays and the Act was to expire on the 31st. December 1904. The Bill passed its first reading on the nod – the written copy was still at the printers – which would seem to imply that Lord Raglan had been both eloquent in his explanations and extremely busy in the lobbies. After lunch, copies were provided and the Members had no difficulty in giving the Bill its second and third readings, although the Attorney General insisted on inserting a clause limiting the cost to the Treasury of such items as the payment of marshals.

Before the Bill could become an Act and therefore the "Law of the Land" there were still two very important steps to be taken. The King had to give his Assent and this he duly did at Buckingham Palace on the 28th. March 1904. Once returned to the Island with the Royal Assent, Tynwald under ancient tradition had to communicate the fact to the Manx nation. Even in this modern age of the 1990's, new Acts are promulgated from Tynwald Hill every 5th. July.

There was an exception in 1904 however, with the trials scheduled for 10th. May, the promulgation of the Act was needed before the usual Tynwald Day ceremony at St.Johns. Arrangements were put in hand and the entire Legislature of the Isle of Man travelled by automobile and train to St.Johns on the 5th. May. For many members of the Keys and Legislative Council this was to be their first experience of riding in an automobile. It was fitting that Mr. Orde had organised a fleet of vehicles to convey the more adventurous souls to the West of the Island.

Rain fell throughout the journey. There was a rush by members to purchase cloth caps for fear that their traditional bell-toppers be swept away in the draught caused by the swiftly moving machines. After a church service in the Royal Chapel, they proceeded to promulgate the Act by reading it aloud in Manx and English to those assembled at Tynwald Hill. The way was now clear for the British to challenge for the honours that must surely come their way.

Shortly after the first trials were completed in the Island the Gordon Bennett Race took place in Germany. Arrangements were, as they had been previously in France, less than efficient and the first suggestions of having a permanent home for British Motorsport were beginning to surface.

The decision to repeat the Trial became a formality because of the overwhelming welcome and assistance that had been given to Orde and his colleagues the previous year. Race fever was now beginning to appeal to the British public's imagination; a permanent venue within easy reach of supporters was essential.

Julian Orde was back on the Island again in the spring of 1905 seeking, in addition, permission for forty cars to race in September. The first Act had been designed to cover any period of up to three days racing in a year. Orde's new suggestion was to extend racing by a further three days later in the year for a new Trophy. The French were not in the least concerned at this provincial challenge to their overall supremacy. How time was to prove their dismissive attitude wrong!

Once again Tynwald was not found wanting and the Island was unanimous in its desire to see Mann become the headquarters of automobile racing. The new Highways (Motor Car) Act 1905 originally with a life span until December 1907, was passed on the 28th. March 1905, achieved Royal Assent on the 10th. May and after promulgation by Deemster Kneen at 11.15 am on 29th. May at St. Johns, the way was clear for the Gordon Bennett trials to commence the next day.

Within the 1905 negotiations an idea surfaced that perhaps the Isle of Man might be just the place to test and improve motorcycles. Considering that the first reliable motorcycle was only sold in 1901, and that between 1902 and 1905 more motorcycles than automobiles were purchased, then the progress of the two wheeled machine had been nothing short of phenomenal. It was no surprise that the Isle of Man wanted to play a leading role in the sport. Provision was sought, and granted, for two of the extra three days to be set aside to conduct motorcycle trials. This arrangement was to prove beneficial in meeting the French challenge. A great debt is owed to whoever was the source of inspiration to hold those early motorcycling trials on the Island.

Still on the Statute Book, in the ninety or so years since its implementation the 1905 Act has rarely been updated, save to keep it in step with modern legislation. Amendment to it has always benefited the TT and other road racing series.

In 1900 when James Gordon Bennett handed over his cup to the Automobile Club of France, his stipulation that the automobile and its component parts, were to be entirely manufactured in the country of origin became the catalyst for the development and perfection of tyres, coils, sparking plugs and electrical accessories. Many of these accessories had been purchased abroad. Now the British had to cease importing and start manufacturing. The experiences of such pioneer racers as Edge had shown that the Continental manufacturers very much had the lead, and a well established one at that, over the British machinery of the day.

Investigation soon showed that development could not move forward apace by simply building automobiles and motorcycles then learning from the experience of the customer. Nor was it simply ever going to be enough for the one man manufacturer to keep abreast of the ever changing improvements continually flooding the market place. In short, if Britain was going to compete seriously and earn for itself a profitable industry, a way must be found to put the stamp of reliability into the manufacture of two and four wheeled vehicles. Development of machines and component parts had to be done under as harsh a regime as possible. It needed a testing ground to provide a broader spectrum of road conditions than the average traveller could expect to meet.

The Isle of Man, it seemed, could fulfil the criteria. It was the start of a love affair between the Island and wheeled sport that has lasted ever since.

GORDON BENNETT   (2)

The Isle of Man in the 1990's has over 1,500 miles of metalled highway. Imagine the situation facing the competitors in the 1904 Gordon Bennett trials. The roads were little better than freshly ploughed fields: horses abounded, livestock, particularly in the lowland areas, wandered without hindrance.

There was however, something different about this small island lying a cosy distance from the shores of England, Ireland, Scotland and Wales. A difference manifesting itself in the welcome given to man and machine. A welcome by sensible laws and legislation and by the people. A welcome to pit their all against the best that Ellan Vannin had to offer ... and that's the way it's been for the racers, their families and supporters ever since.

Searching for a suitable and testing course for the automobiles at first seemed a difficult task but in the end virtually every inch of the Island's official road system, a mere fifty or so miles and, at that, mostly consisting of twin rut track, was used to provide the manufacturers with a wide variety of conditions and gradients as a supreme test of their machinery and equipment. The first course linked most of the main towns and villages, running between Douglas, Ballasalla, Castletown, Foxdale, Ballacraine, Ballaugh, St.Judes and Ramsey before climbing over the Mountain road back to Douglas.

The route was to commence in Douglas and travel in an anti-clockwise direction via Laxey to Ramsey. After inspection in the last week in March 1904 by various dignitaries, including Lord Raglan, Julian Orde, and the Chief Constable, it was decided that the preferred route would be one running in a clockwise direction, omitting Laxey and returning over the Mountain. This route had the decided advantage of avoiding the most heavily populated areas, minimising the dangers to the public. It was also a route that would be a test of careful driving and brake manipulation, rather than of extreme speed. Recommendations were made at this time as to where improvements could be made and barricades erected for reasons of public safety.

Quarterbridge was decided upon as the best place to start the Trial. From here the competitors travelled through meadowland before almost immediately commencing a climb to the summit of Richmond Hill at 471 feet above sea level, approximately two and a half miles from the start. From Newtown the road descended through farmland for the next four and a half miles to Ballasalla and the first checkpoint. Leaving the checkpoint behind, Castletown was reached by passing Ronaldsway farm and King Williams College. This flat country presented ideal conditions to make up for any lost time. Shortly after crossing over the Silver Burn the route swung northwards for the first time and once through Cross-Four Ways the long haul up the Ballamodha Straight began. After climbing for over four miles from some seventy feet above sea level the intrepid trialists had now reached an altitude of almost seven hundred feet.

The first real test of brakes and nerves now faced the competitors as they commenced a three mile descent and speed test down through the two Foxdales to Ballacraine.

The dash to Ballacraine was interrupted at the Foxdale railway bridge, considered in those days to be the "danger spot" for the entire course. Flagmen stopped all cars on the approach to the bridge in order for them to negotiate the corner at a safe speed. Ironically, very little improvement was made to that corner for another sixty or so years when a container lorry decided it was time for the bridge to be removed.

Passing through the second checkpoint at Ballacraine, the soon to be famous Ballig bridge was quickly reached. No such thoughts as resting on successful progress so far entered

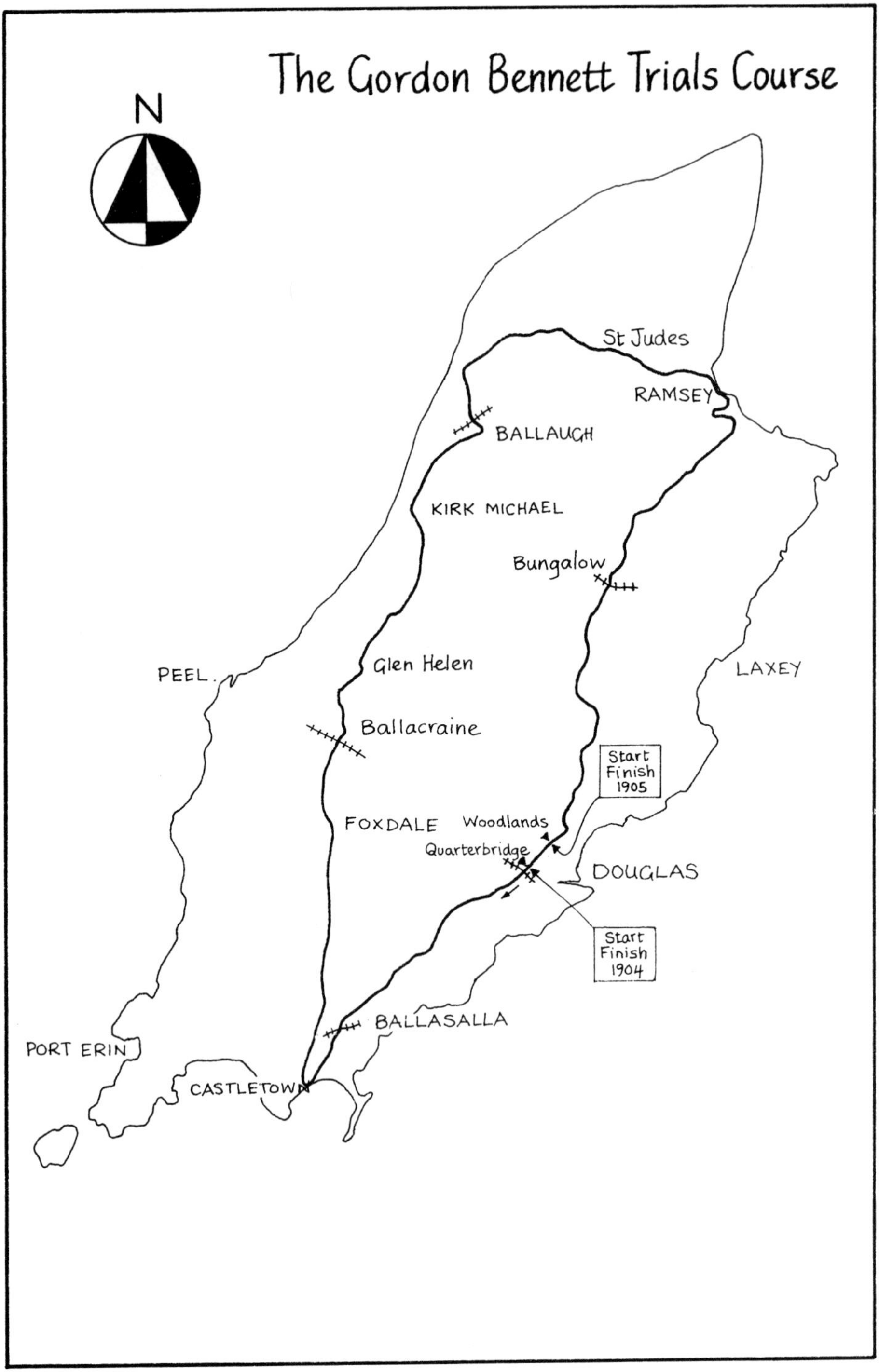
The Gordon Bennett Trials Course
N
St Judes
RAMSEY
BALLAUGH
KIRK MICHAEL
Bungalow
Glen Helen
PEEL
LAXEY
Ballacraine
Start
Finish
1905
FOXDALE
Woodlands
Quarterbridge
DOUGLAS
Start
Finish
1904
BALLASALLA
PORT ERIN
CASTLETOWN

those early pioneers' heads because in no time at all Creg Willey's hill faced them. No trouble to a modern vehicle, maybe, but to the early 1900's drivers a nightmare of a road section rising 300 feet in the space of a half mile!

Four miles of winding country lane brought a slow descent into the lovely village of Kirk Michael, barely changed in almost a century. Just a mile from the village centre the course passed through Rhencullen, hardly in those days harbouring any claims to being one of the fastest sections of the course. Past Bishop's Court to Ballaugh – no airborne thrills here – because race instructions called for a sharp left turn then a trek through Curragh country to St. Judes and onwards to Ramsey. This part of the course for one mile after the Cronk was used as a compulsory speed test: any lost time could usually be regained because it was almost entirely level countryside gently falling from a mere 90 feet above sea level at Ballaugh to the low spot of the course, less than 20 feet in Ramsey's Parliament Square.

Man and machine certainly needed the check point in Parliament Square. They were about to face the toughest test. Designed to force the automobile to the very limits of its capability and the driver to the extreme edge of his ability – the Mountain was the ultimate challenge. It offered no hiding place for the faint hearted. They either made it over the mountain or they didn't. Such was the overall importance of success in the trials to those early manufacturers that it meant the difference between sales and no sales. Slogging up the mountain on what was little better than a sheep track certainly placed stress on the automobile. The development of machines, their parts and the future prosperity of the manufacturers, certainly owed a lot to the knowledge gleaned from the experiences of what was eventually to become the TT course. Faced with an eight mile grind to the highspot of Brandywell, 1384 feet above sea level, there was certainly time to think about their achievement and plan for the next few laps.

With eleven cars in that very first year racing around the Island at great speed, the safety of the public was deemed paramount, none more so than at the Bungalow, where it was anticipated that large crowds would gather courtesy of the Snaefell Mountain Railway. We sense the reader's question. How did the railway passengers safely cross the course? . . . simple, those intrepid railway mountaineers had thought of this . . . . they dug a tunnel!

(Manx National Heritage)

The descent over the next six miles certainly offered a true test of those early braking systems. Downhill all the way to the Hillberry, a drop of 1000 feet in just about four miles, then a stiffish climb up to Cronk-ny-Mona before veering off right down to Johnny Watterson's Lane. Back to civilisation now with a quick sprint along Ballanard Road. Turning sharp right the machines travelled through an area known locally as Siberia, now the site of St. Ninian's High School. The finishing line was almost in sight but first the obstacle of Bray Hill had to be safely overcome. In those far off days its steep gradient offered a fine test of nerve and skill to the driver. Down through open fields lined with spectators, the true spectacle of the trial reached its peak as those early automobiles reached undreamed of speeds in their final thrust for the finishing line alongside the Governor's temporary residence at Woodlands ... and so on to the next lap.

Great was the excitement on the Island as the Trial dates approached. Whilst the major part of the event was the endurance test there was also a hill climb at Port-e-Vullen, Maughold and a speed trial along Douglas promenade. From these three tests Great Britain's representatives for the June 17th. Gordon Bennett Race in Germany would be chosen.

The organisers faced what must at first have seemed to be a quagmire of problems for which there could be no easy solution. Solving problems seems almost to have become an art with the organisers of the TT over the decades. The ease with which its success is achieved lies firmly in the roots of the event, stretching right back to the initial efforts and teamwork of those early years.

Only in the final countdown days to that first Gordon Bennett Eliminating Trial, were people beginning to realise that the organisation had to be right. Few were aware of the importance of such matters as public behaviour around the course during the racing, interruptions to the Island's normal way of life, medical assistance, road surfaces, essential supplies such as spare parts, tyres, fuel, oil and a whole galaxy of problems which if left unattended could mean the failure of the Trials. The Island solved all the problems facing the event and hopes were high that if a British driver secured victory in Germany, the Isle of Man itself could host the 1905 Race and perhaps be selected as a possible venue for the holding of all automobile speed and endurance events.

Bearing in mind the that the length of the course would require a large number of officials to control the general public, livestock and their owners, Lord Raglan issued instructions to recruit five hundred men at five shillings per man. Of course, as ever, Treasury would be keeping an eye on expenditure: this first trial proved to be no different than any of the other events that followed along in the next almost ninety years.

To find suitable persons to marshal the course on a small island was never going to be easy. Fortunately, at that time there was a strong Royal Naval Reserve presence on the Isle of Man. Acknowledging the fine qualities of seamanship displayed over the centuries by the Manx nation, His Britannic Majesty encouraged a state of preparedness in this minute part of the Empire. Anticipating a call to arms was one thing, guarding stretches of road armed only with a whistle and flag was not, it seems, part of King's Regulations.

Self-disciplined and able to conduct themselves with dignity seem to be the main qualifications by which marshals were chosen. Naturally, the naval reservists fell within these criteria but they were never going to be available in sufficient numbers to satisfy Lord Raglan's instructions. On an island that still depended on fishing and farming as its main sources of income there appeared little chance that the shortfall could readily be made up. Then someone remembered the miners! Nothing could be better than to involve the Foxdale miners in the racing. Were they not used to working in an organised industry? An industry where safety was paramount and discipline a pre-requisite to teamwork. So eighty seven miners climbed on board. The remainder of the crew was made up of farmers, their sons and hired hands.

The swearing in of the Foxdale miners as special constables by Mr.W.A. Hutchinson JP MHK in 1904. (Manx National Heritage)

Entries for the 1904 Trial had produced eleven automobiles; five Napiers, three Wolseleys and three Darracqs. As the thrill of Race day grew nearer, so too did the anxiety of the manufacturers. Would their machinery be up to the vagrancies that the course would throw at them? With six rounds of the course planned, the eight hour allowance for the Race appeared sufficient. The results would show that it was hardly generous.

The Gordon Bennett trials were designed to prove which country had developed the best automobile so it may come as something of a surprise to learn that three French designed Darracqs were entered.

Drawings for the cars had been dispatched to Messrs G. and J. Weir of Cathcart, Glasgow. Not a great deal of time was given to manufacture the cars and parts from scratch, but the versatile Scots came up trumps ... and this was the first time any of them had built a car. Before work could start all measurements had to be converted to the British Whitworth system. Patterns and moulds had to be manufactured. This took two weeks, leaving only two months to manufacture four cars – one was for use as a spare – and get them to London for the official weigh-in. Weirs' loyal staff responded magnificently, working day and night, seven days a week, with at times as many as one hundred and fifty men employed on the project. The machines were completed in time, but only just.

Moving the cars to London was a very intricate operation requiring the facility to keep working on them to the last possible moment. No expense had been spared thus far. These Darracqs were probably the most expensive cars ever built. The company was not going to be defeated by a few hours and a mere four hundred miles. Men and machines were loaded on to a special train the evening before the weigh-in which was scheduled to start at noon on the 16th. April 1904. By working through the night on the journey to London, the finishing touches were completed. Mr. Rawlinson, who had supervised the work on behalf of the Darracq Company, was fulsome in his praise of Weirs and their staff. The eyes of Scotland were firmly fixed on the performance of the cars.

The weigh-in was conducted with a great deal of attention to detail, setting standards of inspection which still apply. The examination took a full three days and most machines came through with flying colours, the only exception being a slight overweight problem with the Darracqs. A well handled hacksaw on the exhaust-system and the removal of the bonnet soon brought things back within the set limits and thus guaranteed the car its popular nick name – "the Snorter." Even if the spectators were not going to see much of the car, they would certainly be hearing it.

"Darracq" (Manx National Heritage)

Moving the eleven cars and support teams over to the Island for the Trials scheduled for the 10th., 11th. and 12th. May started almost immediately the weigh-in was finished. This presented no particularly great difficulty to the Isle of Man Steam Packet Company. It was, after all, merely a dress rehearsal for all the years that were to follow.

Pre race checks included re-weighing the cars on Douglas Quay, a short hop from Quarterbridge. The start of the course was the Quarterbridge side of the level crossing on the new Castletown road. Cars were marshalled in race order just around the corner in Peel Road, from where they were instructed to start up and called forward to await the flag. The dignitaries, timekeepers, judges, marshals, flagmen and the starter were all gathered here.

Monsieur Henri sat tensely behind the wheel of one of the three powerful Darracqs. Orde, who spoke some French went to instruct Henri in his own tongue and tried to convey that now was the time for him to start up and roll to the line. Something was lost in the translation! Henri nodded, but it could only have been out of politeness at Orde's best efforts.

Henri's boot hit the board . . . and the Darracq thundered around the corner into the Castletown road. Fortunately the starting party were quick witted and agile enough to leap into the bushes bordering the start.

The first start at Quarterbridge. (Manx National Heritage)

Julian Orde almost forgot he was a gentleman for a few moments. When order was restored, he remembered that he had taken up an offer to set up a series of telephones around the course – was this the first sponsorship deal? A messenger was despatched to telephone the Ballasalla check point to stop Henri and tell him to return to Douglas and start again.

By now Henri had the bit between his teeth. The messenger returned with the information that Henri had passed through Ballasalla faster than anyone else. Obviously the Darracq was shifting. He flew past Ballacraine. Julian Orde decided to let him go. Once past Ballacraine there was no better return road than the course itself.

Henri was in line for a stupendous lap record when on the Mountain section an oil pipe sheared. Somehow, with Gallic courage and despite being covered in oil, he managed, with screaming gears and next to no brakes, to tour the machine back to Peel Road for repairs. Having had the drive of his life, he was greeted by the officials at the finishing line who informed him that he had been disqualified as a result of his flying start.

Witnesses to the final episode were clearly able to see his great distress and distinguish the lack of charitable feelings towards Mr. Orde.

Girling passing St. Olave's Church, Ramsey. (George Gelling)

The first six home were the only six to finish. To Girling driving a Wolseley, fell the honour of recording the fastest round in 1hr.16m.30 secs. Two other notable rounds were put in by Jarrot's Wolseley in 1hr.17m.30 secs and with a time just 3 minutes slower than Jarrot, Hargreaves upheld the honour of the Napier stable. The end of Race placings showed that the first and last of the finishers in the endurance trial were only separated by just over a half hour.

First	– number 6,	Earp	Napier,	7 hrs.26m – 30 secs.
Second	– number 10,	Girling	Wolseley,	7 hrs.30m
Third	– number 9,	Edge	Napier,	7 hrs.33m – 40 secs.
Fourth	– number 1,	Stocks	Napier,	7 hrs.46m – 30 secs.
Fifth	– number 12,	Jarrot	Wolseley,	7 hrs.52m – 10 secs.
Sixth	– number 3,	Hargreaves	Napier,	7 hrs.57m

Of the Darracqs, alas no sign! What a disappointment this must have been for those creative Scots engineers who put in such a valiant effort. Alexandre Darracq suffered not only disappointment but financial loss. So determined was he to win the Gordon Bennett Race in 1904, that he entered three cars in the French eliminatoire and sponsored three Opel built Darracqs in the German Trial. Out of all these cars only one, an Opel-Darracq survived the trials to reach the start line at Bad Homburg; even that did not survive the first lap.

The following day's hill climb from Port-e-Vullen to Maughold church had a short lived existence being the one and only occasion it was used as part of the Gordon Bennett selection process. The result was:

1. Edge, 2. Earp, 3. Girling, 4. Jarrot, 5. Campbell-Muir (Wolseley), 6. Hargreaves, 7. Stocks.

The Douglas sprint on the 12th. May proved to be a spectacular event but probably sowed the seeds of doubt in the minds of the more cautious members of the Island's Highway Board that high speed automobiles and the general public should be kept as far apart as possible. Edge won again chased home again by Earp and in third place the valiant Girling in his Wolseley.

The Gordon Bennett result for 1904 had Edge, Girling and Jarrot selected for the team with Hargreaves and Stocks as reserves. At the end of a splendid three days of Trials Julian Orde and his colleagues were satisfied that they had chosen the very best team to represent King and Country . . . . or so it seemed.

Dissent and storm clouds were swiftly gathering.

S.F. Edge at Port Lewaigue. (George Gelling)

Earp had not been chosen for either the team or as one of the reserves. His omission from the team was perhaps a hasty decision based purely on the fact that he had crashed on returning for the third leg of the Douglas Sprint injuring himself and damaging the car. Both driver and vehicle swiftly recovered from their injuries. Edge lodged an unsuccessful protest about Earp's non-selection and as a consequence withdrew. Jarrot appears to have had difficulty in representing Britain and the reserves stepped down, leaving only Girling to represent the country.

When it was all over the five-bob whistlemen went back to fishing, farming and mining. Each had played his part. Fear of the unknown had been conquered to be replaced by fierce pride. Pride that they had been involved in an event that was to catapult their island into a position of world prominence.

As those stalwarts made their way home, the Isle of Man was already beginning to bathe in the glory of those wonderful men and their racing machines. Whilst it would have been difficult for the volunteer element to judge the effect on the economy, those in government were cheered by the benefits accruing to Mona's Isle. Success was being measured not in column inches or even yards but in the miles and miles of newsprint devoted to the story of the Gordon Bennett Trial by newspapers and magazines on a provincial, national and worldwide basis. The publicity generated from this one event was as if the Isle of Man was the Moon and Man had just taken his first nervous steps on the surface.

Motor Tynwald Day.

The Legislature Ride to Tynwald Hill in Motor Cars.

THURSDAY, MAY 5th, 1904.

Tempora mutantur nos et mutamur in illis! Recognising the truth in this old Latin wisdom, we can imagine the sober-side old members of the Legislature, who had choice of several modes of conveyance to Tynwald Hill on Thursday last, ex-promulgation of the Motor Race Act, exclaiming with a further use of foreign, "Tempori parentum," and yielding to the seduction of a ride thither in a motor car. Thirty years ago our legislators first rode to Tynwald Hill by railway, the trains on which, then as now, ran at the maximum speed of thirty miles an hour. The legislators have talked as if perfect in dynamo mechanics had been attained. A generation has passed, and some of those legislators—the road forgotten the rail for the olden days, then tra-over which, in the means of travel is ruled to Tynwald, either in horsed vehicle or on foot—though the method having still mechanical, only the years ago, after look-changed. Thirty years ago, after looking at a Manx express travelling along its set course of iron rails, no one dreamt that a machine, an old-style side-car for size, would be invented which would travel along the old-time highroad at a speed at-taining to ninety miles an hour. But in the short period intervening this seeming impossibility has been achieved, and people in this age have become so accus-tomed to wonders that they hardly ever are to be caught expressing the surprise of wonderment. The Isle of Man having been selected as the place for the Gordon-Bennett Motor Race Eliminating Trials, and an Act having to be obtained to en-able racing on the highroads, a special Tyn-wald Day had to be promulgated. It was very fitting that for such an occasion the Act might have been considerate to pass a special measure, should have been given the opportunity of riding by motor car to Tynwald Hill for the Motor Act ceremony. It was made known to the members of the Legislature at the sitting on Tuesday that Mr Orde, the secretary of the Automobile Club, had arranged to con-from Douglas to Tynwald, all such as desire to experience motor travel Most of the members reading on this side of the Island notified their wishfulness to have a first motor ride, and to this end met in front of the Legislative Buildings at half-past ten on Thursday morning. Mr Hutchinson, the member for Middle, who had already performed the service of swear-ing in 500 special constables through the Island, to serve on the day of the ceremonies, and assist to control the course, was mak-

after hearing Miss ... with the consent of ... did not feel inclined to ... make Miss Marsden ... than Miss Fletcher. ... come to this—that the ... teachers to go from one ... He thought teachers ... ferred without being asked. ... teachers of the Board. The policy ... being introduced was a bad one. ... particular school. They had no ... being introduced. It was merely ... the motion. That was why they had not ... for a teacher.

... for the ... of changing an older for a youn-teacher. Mr Douglas wished to express his decided ... objection to teachers being allowed to dio-... in this fashion. Whether Mr Knoale ... solicited the letter he did not know, but it was a pity a private letter should come before the Board. Mr Carine said Mr Kerruish had asked to withdraw the motion, and therefore further discussion was out of order. The matter then dropped.

SPECIAL HOLIDAYS FOR THE MOTOR RACES.

Mr Kerruish, as a matter of urgency, asked leave to move that the schools of the Board be closed on Tuesday, the 10th, on account of the motor races. Their position was thus: In the year, counting this holiday and the 12th of May and Whit-Monday, they would have made 416 at-tendances. The ... of ... Council of Education within the limit. They were well to attempt to open the day of the motor race. There would be futile ... attendance from the race-cars, on bring for-complete ... police arrange ... be h ... that they ... inspector of the ...

---

stallions ... man in o2-... the horses show ... have done at a p... deed, the fact was made ... a cable car, or even a horse, ... spires fear in many horses. The members of the ... is a thing they will pass without a ... of fear or agitation. The Governor, however, set Council all rode to Tynwald in a motor ... veyances. The example of Mr Orde, and arrived from time to time. As usual, there was a He travelled with Mr Orde, and arrived prompt to time. As usual, there was a Tynwald Day, the 5th of July, under Lieut. the full ceremonial performance, Lieut. fifty Naval Reserve men, under Cowle, Newham, and the Douglas Volunteers, under Capt. Mackenzie and Lieut. His formed the guard of honour to receive Excellency. The motorists present, of whom there were about 60, were the most interested spectators of the ceremony. Every item they sought, explanation of. The Governor on passing to the church for Divine service, received the Royal Salute from both soldiers and sailors, and once representative of His Majesty, and once within the church portals the National Anthem kept up the strain of the National Anthem till he had taken his stall in the chancel. The service was conducted by the Govern-ment chaplains, the Rev. J. Corlett and the Rev. F. H. Loatham Locke, the latter rea-ing the prayers and the former the less-The singing was lead by choristers of Church.

THE PROMULGATION.

Immediately on the conclusio service, Police Superintendent the order of procession to Tyn This was as follows:—

Four Sergeants of ...
The Coro...
(Messrs J. Kennedy, ...
Kermode, P. Teare ...
ruish, and Ch...
Captains o...
(Dr Tellett, and ...
Bacon, D. Te...
J. Q. Canne...
Th...
(The Revs J. ...
Taggart, ...
Walmsley ...
Kinred ...
Tyler ...
(Ma...
(Mo...

Mona's Herald 11th. May 1904.

22

THE WAY FORWARD (3)

Although far from pleased with the British performance in the 1904 Gordon Bennett Trial, the Automobile Club of Great Britain and Ireland was already planning the way forward. Orde was soon back on the Island, encouraging his cousin and the multitude of converts to motorsport that the Isle of Man had a leading role to play in the development of the racing machine. He must have had a feeling that the days of the Gordon Bennett Trial were numbered. Not wishing to see the progress of the all-British car and motorcycle halted, his proposal to run a touring car race for a new prize called the Tourist Trophy in addition to the Gordon Bennett Trial was eagerly seized upon.

Utilising the extra days of racing granted under The Highways (Motor Car) 1905 Act appeared to be as good a means as any to continue the development of the "home grown" machines. Orde opened discussions with all interested parties including the members of Douglas Corporation and the Advertising Board as to when the most advantageous dates would be to run this event, the forerunner of the TT. Owing to the harvest and a desire to extend the holiday season, 9.00 a.m. Thursday 14th. September 1905 was the chosen start time and date.

The route would be the one used for the Gordon Bennett Eliminating Trials, by now known as the highroad course, but there would be no check points. The cars would only be required to complete four laps of the circuit, a total distance of 203 miles 4 furlongs. A basic system of control by means of flag signals was devised; drivers were notified that observers would be stationed at strategic positions around the course to ensure compliance. Speeds would be reasonably reduced and no overtaking permitted when passing between the red flags marking the entrance and exit to villages. For the first time machines would have their race number compulsorily displayed.

As a further improvement the 1905 start line was moved to the junction of Alexander Drive and Quarterbridge Road and the the first Grandstand built. It seems the lesson of M. Henri had been well heeded. Total control of the start and finish area was imperative and all the evidence indicates a desire to have a top speed finish on a straight line. The 1905 finish was just past the junction of Selborne Drive and Quarterbridge Road.

Since there were to be no control or check points around the course it was felt that average speeds and risks to competitors would rise. Accordingly in September 1905 the number of ambulance stations was increased to twenty.

There was however a landmark event that took place prior to the September Tourist Trophy Race that probably caused more excitement and captured the attention of the populace in a way that no previous activity had managed.

In response to a desire to challenge the French it was decided to run a trial for motor-cycles on the 31st. May 1905, the day after the Gordon Bennett Car Trials. From the finishers a team to represent Great Britain in the forthcoming international races in France, would be chosen. The Trials would be run under the auspices of the Auto-Cycle Club, later to become the Auto-Cycle Union, the start of a continuing relationship.

By now, ever keen to prove the superiority of British machinery, there was little doubt in the minds of the organisers that the highroad course would be an ideal proving ground. However, a pre-race accident at Ramsey Hairpin to the favourite, J.F, Crundall, one of the best riders in the country, forced a last minute change. The "new" motorcycle course followed the route of the Trial course as far as Ballacraine where the riders then turned back towards Douglas. In a sense, although they were unaware of it at the time, they were breaking trail for the TT course of 1911, albeit in the opposite direction.

1905 Auto Cycle Trial

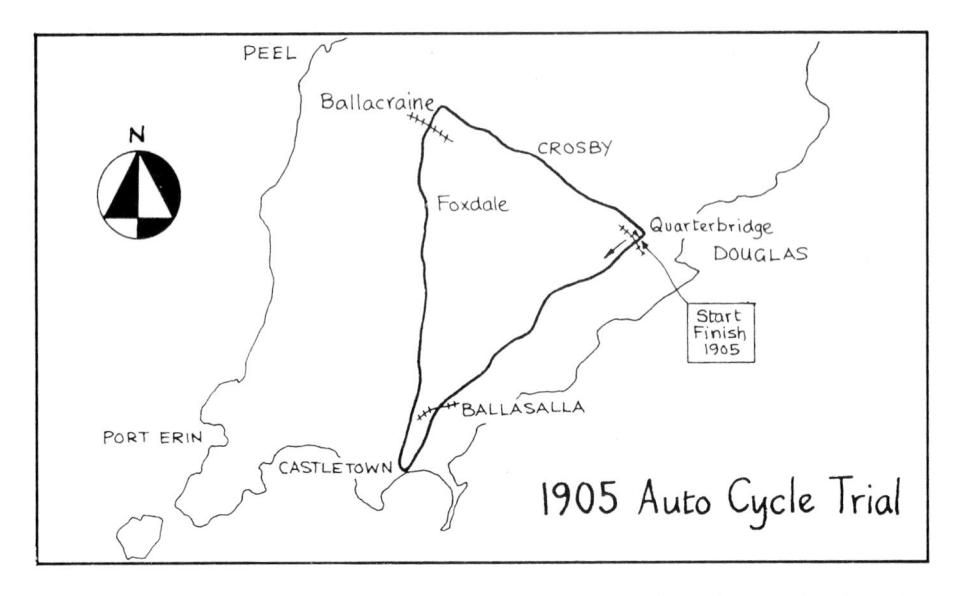

When Race day dawned only the English pressmen grumbled about the unearthly hour that the trial was scheduled to start, 3-00 a.m.*. They soon cheered up when informed that the bar was open in the Quarterbridge Hotel. No such grumbles from the enthusiastic Manx, the organisers and indeed six out of the seventeen entrants . . . you see they were all up and ready to go. Spectators, bright eyed and bushy tailed were already perched in trees, on hedges and all the best vantage points much to the chagrin of the bleary eyed pressmen. It didn't seem to matter too much that the remaining riders eventually awoke from their slumbers and staggered to the start, to be sent on their way with a cheery word or two.

The trial was won by J.S. Campbell in 4h.9m.36 secs, who was followed home by H. Collier – the first of many times this famous name was to feature on the rostrum – in a time of 4hrs.10m.5 2/5th.secs. Both riders having completed five out of the maximum seven rounds within the time allowed were subsequently chosen to represent their country in the French race.

For the gentlemen of the press there remained one more dramatic story to write. In the early hours of that Wednesday morning, as the motorcycles were jostling for position, the official results of the previous day's Gordon Bennett Trial were announced. In first place Clifford Earp (Napier), Second the Hon. C.S. Rolls (Wolseley); in third place Bianchi (Wolseley). Uproar ensued! Even today there still remains conjecture as to why Bianchi was deprived of second place when only he and Earp completed all six laps.

By the time September arrived the idea of a Tourist Trophy Race, open to all, had certainly captured the imagination of the British motoring enthusiast. Entries poured in. With over fifty cars entered, the Secretary of the event, non other than Julian Orde issued instructions that the weigh-in and examination of the vehicles would commence at 10.00 a.m. on Monday 11th. September. The Automobile Club set up a temporary garage at Selborne Road, utilising two large marquees to store the cars until race day.

Orde himself had set up headquarters in the Peveril Hotel, now the site of a huge office block. From here he controlled proceedings: the Peveril must have been a scene of frantic activity as race day drew near.

* Times were GMT in those days and therefore there would have been daylight.

The Race was to be decided by speed and fuel consumption. Once each car had taken its quota the tanks were locked and sealed. The Race regulations stipulated that each car would be permitted to carry an allowance of 9 gallons and 1 quart of fuel at a retail cost of one shilling (5p) per gallon.

By now the magnitude of the event had begun to sink in with the powers that be. Instructions were being issued at regular intervals by Chief Constable Freeth to his corps of special constables to ensure that they paid extra vigilance in seeing the roads were kept clear and authorising them to permit householders, who had made special application, to cross the course in order to reach their dwellings. The Highway Board had their steam rollers working on the course . . . and so the guidelines even in 1905 were beginning to set a pattern that over the years would be honed to perfection. The generations that followed simply accepted the instructions as part of the norm and got on with ensuring that the TT was the best run event of its kind in the world.

Thursday 14th. September 1905 was a day to mark in the annals of Manx History. Setting off from 9.00 a.m. at one minute intervals, the cars began their progress around the course. Early reports began to be phoned in. The Hon. C.S. Rolls had broken his gear box on Richmond Hill. Downie driving the Argyll had crashed into the Whitestone Inn at Ballasalla. A. Lee Guinness's Darracq was reported to have retired at Ramsey with a burst tyre and broken spoke. The smallest car in the race, the Cadillac driven by F.S. Bennett suffered a shift of ballast at Creg-ny-Baa, which caused the car to break up and the driver to be deposited in a turnip field. This particular bend for a while was known as Bennett's Bend, the first recorded instance of part of the course being named after a competitor.

F.S. Bennett at Crosby in 1955 being re-united with an original part of his 1905 car.
(George Gelling)

A disaster nearer home came at 10.00 a.m. when an official car being driven along Selborne Road towards the course ran over three children. First aid was rendered by Inspector Cain whilst two of the children were whisked off to hospital for treatment. The third child, Master John Corkill of Hawarden Avenue made light of his injuries and sped off to find another vantage spot. If he had guessed that he could have had a ride in a car, then he too would have opted for a visit to hospital.

At 12.10 p.m. the first lap, or as they called it in those days, the first round, was completed by Guy Baxendale's Thorneycroft. As he went past the start point, surprised officials saw the mechanic exhibiting a burst tyre, which obviously accounted for their last place.

With retirements in each of the four laps the course was taking its toll and proving its worth to the manufacturers. The eighteen finishers had done extremely well. The cars in their final finishing order were;

First   – number 53, an Arrol-Johnston with 1 gallon 6 ozs of fuel remaining.
Second – number 22, the second string Rolls-Royce with 3 quarts left.
Third   – number 52, the only Vinot-Deguingand in the race.
Fourth – number 54, the second Arrol-Johnston.
Fifth   – number 49, Rover, with another Rover coming in twelfth.
Sixth   – number 25, a Swift.
Seventh – number 8, an Orleans with the other half of the pair coming in ninth.
Eighth – number 18, the remaining Argyll.

The famous Napiers didn't have such a good race but at least they finished a respectable tenth and fifteenth. History was also made in the race with a lady finisher. Number 35, a Dennis designed and driven by Mr R Dennis with his wife in the mechanic's position came in a creditable eighteenth, last but not least amongst equals!

As a footnote to the result and as a lesson for future races, it was alleged in the Manx Sun newspaper of 20th.September 1905, that if the deciding factor had been fuel consumption only and not the combination of speed and fuel used then the positions of the first and last cars would have been reversed.

All in all a very successful first Tourist Trophy Race. Lessons had been learned. Planning for 1906 would get under way shortly and the inhabitants of Ellan Vannin had the winter to reflect on what was to prove for many, the means to a better way of life.

Setting new objectives to improve the racing has long been a yearly target as far as the race organisers have been concerned. Targets do need however a considerable amount of careful planning and for events such as the TT they could never be achieved without dedicated teamwork. Thankfully for all the generations of riders and supporters ever since, this was recognised at an early date. Government, the public, manufacturers, the competitors, and the myriad of race connected satellite services and activities soon became welded into a very fine team.

The Isle of Man Highway Board now known as The Department of Highways, Ports and Properties has for many years devoted part of its road improvement budget to ensuring that the TT course is kept up to scratch: increasing speeds around the course cannot all be laid at the door of the successful development of racing machinery. Quite early on in the saga the importance of better road surfaces was seen as a means of enhancing the meeting. 1905 was the year in which the road surfaces began to come under closer scrutiny. Two experiments were conducted. For the Gordon Bennett Trial, the Liverpool firm R.S. Clare won the right to demonstrate their product, a new dust-laying composition called Dustroyd. The Tourist Trophy Race was to be the proving ground for Westrumite compound laid down by Hope & Sons of Millwall. Naturally by virtue of the length of the course only relatively short sections could be treated, but at least it was a start and it did point the way to the almost billiard table smooth road surfaces that are used nowadays. Racing on public roads was starting to have spin-offs in all sorts of directions.

The two experiments.

(George Gelling) (R. S. Clare & Co.)

In a series of alterations over a comparably short period of time the courses moved away from the south of the Island. After a brief flirtation with the far west the event settled down in 1911 to a more or less permanent home in the north. Many years later the south of the Island was recalled from the wilderness by the introduction of the Southern 100 short circuit.

What started the move away from the South? Surprisingly, it was because of the Railway Companies. With railway lines crossing the Gordon Bennett route at Quarterbridge, Ballasalla, just before Ballacraine, Ballaugh and the Bungalow, both the Isle of Man Railway and the Manx Northern Railway Companies were concerned about the disruption caused to their services during the running of the 1904 and 1905 Gordon Bennett Trials.

The addition of the 1905 Tourist Trophy to the racing calendar and its anticipated popularity with the public led the Companies to provide special express trains for spectators. The express part of the service actually came in the form of an allowance of thirty seconds, in which the train drivers and level crossing keepers had to move an entire train over a crossing. In fairness to the Railway Management they did double bank the trains to speed them up. As a further precaution, if the level crossing keeper saw a competing car approaching, the gates were to be closed against any advancing train. Car drivers were also given a list of crossings and a timetable which were pasted to their dash boards. All seemed under control. Did it work? Did it heck! Events, as they often do, took a turn for the worse. Stories of delayed trains soon filtered back to both Race and Railway HQ's. This was the final straw as far as the Railways were concerned and after a gentlemanly discussion with Orde, the course changed for the 1906 events.

The Snaefell Mountain Railway people must have been aware of the value of the races to their part of the world right from the word go because a wise management saw financial reward in transporting the spectating public up the mountain to what has always been a favourite vantage point at the Bungalow. No matter that the racing machines took a route which bisected their track. No matter that the race took hours to run. The answer was quite simple; they left rolling stock either side of the road.

The only major accident on the Mountain Railway occurred on the 14th. September 1905, the day of that very first Tourist Trophy Race. An ascending tramcar in the vicinity of Lhergy Veg, approximately half way between Laxey and the Bungalow stopped as a consequence of either a motor failure or a loss of wire contact. Descending the track at this time was a convoy of three tramcars and it was a collision between the middle tramcar and the last in line of the convoy that caused the accident. A rear-end collision! Generous compensation was paid to the injured parties seriously affecting the year's profit but did nothing to diminish the enthusiasm of the Railway Company for motor sport. In the intervening years the Railway has continued to play its part, acting at times as ambulance, communicator, supplier of food and beverages, and always there in a supporting role when needed.

The tramcar crash did nothing to reduce the excitement that prevailed after the Tourist Trophy Race had ended that September. Considerable publicity had been generated for the Island and a way forward had now been found to harness everyone's enthusiasm.

Reports of the French and British withdrawal from the 1906 Gordon Bennett Trial coupled with James Gordon Bennett's decision to switch his allegiance to balloon racing caused consternation on the Island. Bennett's change of loyalty, unwelcome news as it was, happily for the Isle of Man had coincided with the successful promotion of the first Tourist Trophy Race. Here was a ready made substitute with a proven record.

Taking into account factors such as Orde's conversation with the railway companies, road surfaces, lap times, public interest, safety and a desire on the part of the organisers to work their way towards the best possible course, a decision was reached. The conclusion that any future races would need to be over a shorter and more manageable route was a wise one. Although history shows that we were still some little way from the course as we now know it, at least the enthusiasts of yesteryear were moving in the right direction.

Bearing in mind that there was to be no Gordon Bennett Trial in 1906 and with the added comfort that the racing on public roads was covered by the Act of Tynwald until the end of 1907 the organisers found themselves provided with that rarest of commodities, time! The worthies of the day did not waste it. This was to be a period of transition in the history of the Race. Choosing a route that maintained all the early principles of the 1904 and 1905 trials remained a priority. Entrants in the 1906 race were not to be disappointed.

Starting from the point adjacent to "Woodlands" in the vicinity of the Quarterbridge Road's junction with Alexander Drive the cars were routed out through Braddan Bridge in exactly the same direction as the modern day course, as far as Ballacraine. Straight on from Ballacraine they raced past St.John's, over the tricky Ballaleece Bridge and across the sandy countryside into Peel. Negotiating a sharp right-hander into Albany Road and then a sharp right-hander out of Church Street the machines climbed out of Peel via Peveril Road (A3).

Two miles out of Peel the cars passed over the Manx Northern Railway Company's St. Germains level crossing. On past Knocksharry, round the Devil's Elbow to Glen Mooar, up the steep climb past Glen Wyllin to the point where the modern course in the shape of the A4 merges into the A3 just a few yards short of the ancient Mitre Hotel, through Kirk Michael, Rhencullen and so to Ballaugh. The fast Ballaugh, St.Judes to Ramsey section was abandoned in favour of the main road through Sulby, Glentramman, Milntown to Ramsey. From Ramsey the course was the same as for the earlier trials.

The set of statistics shown below indicate clearly how closely the course designers were able to adhere to the early race principals and subject the entrants to much the same tests, but over a shorter route.

	1904/5 course	1906 course
Length	52 1/8th.miles	40 3/8th.miles
Distance travelled uphill	21 5/8th.miles	17 2/8th.miles
Average gradient	1 in 35	1 in 37
Distance travelled level	3 3/8th.miles	–
Distance travelled downhill	27 1/8th.miles	23 1/8th.miles
Average gradient	1 in 41	1 in 49

Even before the old year closed, interest in the next Tourist Trophy Race was keen. By September 30th. 1905 fifteen cars had already been entered.

The Hon. C.S.Rolls "felt that by now most cars had become standardised but even so there was still much to be gleaned about a car's performance especially under racing conditions. A race such as the Gordon Bennett had probably outgrown its usefulness for all but the wealthiest of manufacturers." He concluded by stating, "that a race such as the Tourist Trophy would provide as much, if not more development information than its illustrious but expensive predecessor." High praise indeed for the fledgling Race.

1906 saw some of the lessons learned put into good effect with rule changes governing weight, vehicle dimensions, the carriage of spare parts and strict sanctions on the support teams and depots. In short the cars were to be as close to touring cars as possible. Elaborate precautions were also taken to prevent any fraudulent additions to the petrol supply.

In practising a number of cars suffered mishaps and there were injuries, some serious, to various drivers and mechanics. Stories abounded of collisions with animals and birds and an early version of "chicken" seems to have been played by some irresponsible spectators. Destruction of livestock in those days was deemed to be the responsibility of the vehicle only and there were reports circulating on the Island of "much insurance money changing hands."

The weigh-in was not without controversy; a number of cars were disqualified for arriving at the Selborne Road enclosure after the 10:00 a.m. limit.

Well before the appointed starting hour on 27th. September crowds were gathering near the "Woodlands" start. Forty seven entrants had been whittled down by accidents, disqualifications and withdrawals to just thirty one.

1906/7 Car T.T. Course

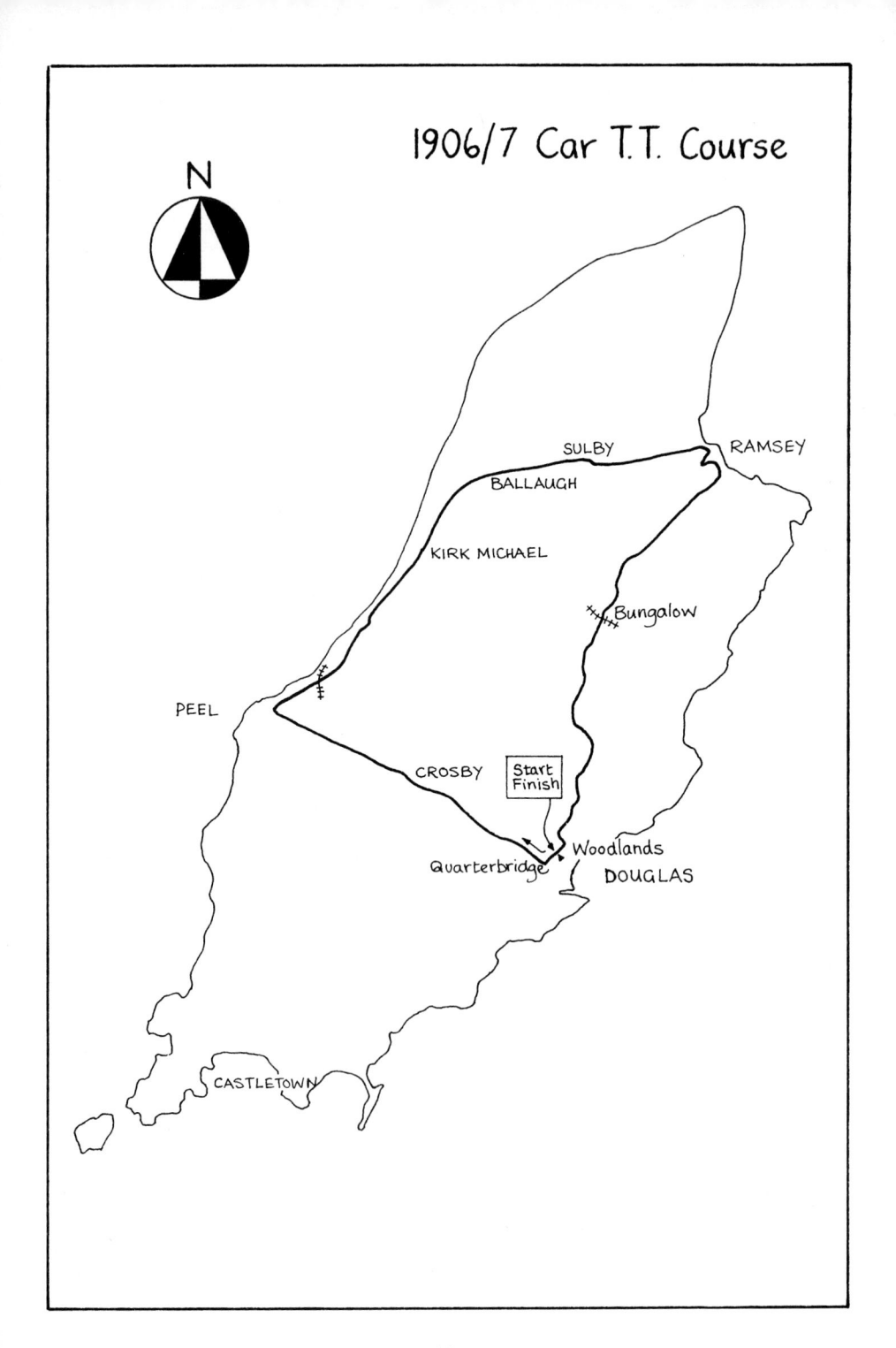

Mr. Napier's Arrol-Johnston, the winner of the 1905 Tourist Trophy was first away, followed at one and a half minute intervals by the rest of the field. Julian Orde was doing a sterling job as starter. As he flagged away car number 4, he perhaps had a suspicion that this might well be the Hon. C.S. Rolls' year.

After the first round only two cars had retired, followed by four more on the second round which was equalled on the penultimate lap. With only ten cars completing the four lap race, the job of re-weighing and calculating the finishing order began shortly before 4:30 p.m. when the last finisher, Mr. Percy Dean's 17 h.p. Scout arrived back in Quarterbridge Road.

Rolls had finished in 4hrs.6m 3/5th. secs and was declared the winner with 0.131 gallons of petrol remaining. Second almost 27 minutes later and with 0.0938 gallons in the tank was number 23, a French Berliet driven by M. Bablot. The last of the top three spots went to car number 2, another French designed car, but built in Scotland. This machine, the sole surviving Darracq driven by Mr. A. Lee Guinness came in a respectable 9m.50 secs behind number 23 and with 0.0656 of a gallon of fuel remaining.

Mr. Alec Govan's Argyll driven by George was disqualified on the grounds that the car had not completed the full distance in racing trim. On the second round the latches holding part of the car's floor in place had given way, depositing sand ballast, coats and rugs on to the road. It mattered not that he picked it all up again on the third round.

Out of the original forty seven entries there were 13 French made or designed cars, twenty three British, three Belgian, three Italian and five privateers. Britain claimed six out of the nine places with the French contained to only three, but they were the prestigious second, third and fourth.

Looking at the lap times for this, the second Tourist Trophy Race, it appears that most of the cars had discovered their limits. Many of the cars show very similar times for each of their rounds. The winning Rolls-Royce for instance recorded times of:

First Round	1h.0m. 13 secs
Second Round	1h.0m. 46 secs
Third Round	1h.1m. 24 secs
Fourth Round	1h.3m. 36 secs

A good effort for those days, but only a taste of what was to come in the future, when motorcycle races would be decided on split seconds even after travelling upwards of two hundred miles. Already the British manufacturers were beginning to reap the development benefits that the Isle of Man races were providing: twenty six cars, over half the field, raced on Dunlop tyres.

Control and entertainment of spectators was becoming an art form with Police, Marshals and Stewards all developing crowd management skills. Entertainment in plenty there was not, but to help in whiling away the time until the official results were announced, the Automobile Club had secured the services of the Douglas Volunteer Band. A more exciting form of entertainment was provided by a Hot Air Balloon, which had been operating out of the Palace grounds during the practice period and which had been attached to the Grandstand for the Race. Used as a means of raising funds for Noble's Hospital it received great attention, but there was a slight hiccup when a couple of sandbags broke loose – perhaps Bungie Jumping is not so dangerous as it appears!

That Thursday evening the crowds gathered in the Palace ballroom to greet the hero of the day, the Hon. C.S. Rolls. Making his entrance shortly before 9:00 p.m., the dancing stopped and he was given a rapturous welcome. Lord Raglan presented Rolls with the trophy. Rolls paid tribute to his mechanic, the designer and the manufacturer, a tradition that exists to this very day.

On the subject of traditions, many compliments were paid to the voluntary helpers after the 1906 Race. There must have been a temptation to gain the best vantage spots. Volunteers were made of stronger stuff and would not be diverted from their task by mere personal advantage ... and so it is today, with a fourth generation of volunteers from those same dedicated families from on and off the Island, doing their bit for the races.

In the cold light of day after the winding down process of the Race had been completed it was back on with the thinking caps to plan for next year. Changes were to be expected; 1907 was to be no exception.

During the annual dinner of the Auto-Cycle Club held in London on the 17th. January 1907 the Editor of "The Motor Cycle" proposed a competition for motor-cycles, run on similar lines to the car TT. Shortly before that, disenchantment with the International Cup Races held on the continent since 1903 had reached boiling point. Frustrated by the lack of trials on the Isle of Man in springtime, 1906 – the demise of the Gordon Bennett Trials meant that there had been no event on which to piggy-back them – a scratch team set off for Austria in poor spirits. Shenanigans and accusations of downright cheating conspired to lead the team to discuss alternatives for the following year. On the long journey back home the Collier brothers, Freddie Straight, Secretary of the Auto-Cycle Club and the Marquis de Mouzilly St. Mars, an anglophile if ever there was one, pooled their ideas to lay the foundations of what would become the first TT for motorcycles. Not quite as slick tyred as the Manx Politicians of less than two years before, it is nevertheless a credit to the Auto-Cycle Club that the suggestion bore fruit on Tuesday 28th. May 1907.

1907 AND ALL THAT! (4)

Freddie Straight's anticipation in devising a complete set of regulations during 1906 to govern the racing of touring motorcycles was to be the springboard into 1907 and the Isle of Man Tourist Trophy. The arguments about the length of the course, engine capacities, weight limits, silencers, size of tyres, spares, pedals, saddles and even the style of mudguards were as many as they were varied and a solution seemed a long way off. Straight came up with an answer of such simplicity that all discussion quickly ceased. Arguing that fuel consumption alone should be the deciding factor seemed an ideal method well worthy of adoption. Considering that with just over eighteen weeks in total to prepare for the Race there must have been a sense of relief for everyone when agreement was reached with only six weeks to go. Agreement meant that the Race was to be a two class affair with one competition for single-cylinder machines averaging 90 m.p.g. being run concurrently with a competition for multi-cylinder machines averaging 75 m.p.g.

Straight was worried about choosing a route that would be too long and so testing that there would be no finishers. The St. John's circuit was chosen as the best route embodying, as it did, all the principles leading to the furthering of machine development over a shorter but just as demanding a course. It was a drop down from a marathon course to an almost modern style of short circuit, but at least it would give the spectators a chance to study riders and machines on a more regular basis than on the, by now, traditional Gordon Bennett course.

Finding a suitable position for the start and finish lines presented no difficulties. Tynwald Fair Field was ideal – plenty of room for officials, riders, motorcycles, mechanics and spectators. The paddock was alongside the wall removed some years ago to make way for a car park adjacent to the Tynwald Inn. Whilst the TT has never been able to reach the heights of sophistication in scoreboards, they have always managed to be adequate for the purpose. Setting standards was always important, styles not so much. The 1907 scoreboard was never likely to to set a trend but the blackboards from the village school were up to the task.

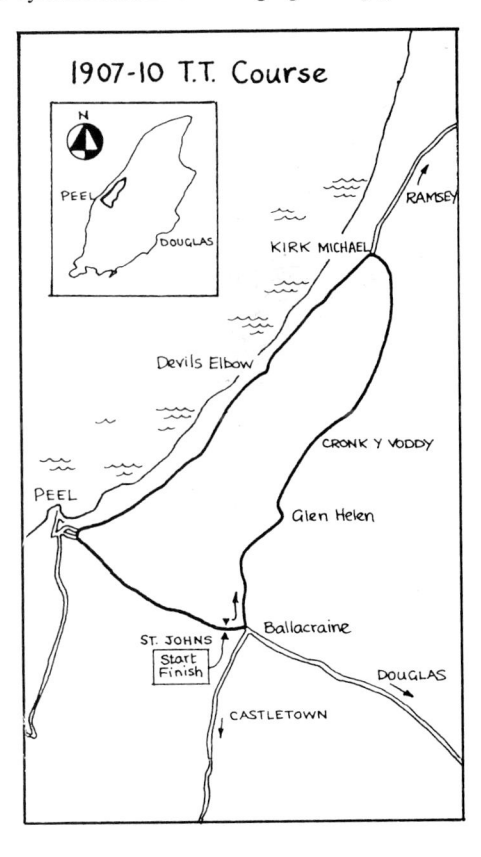

1907-10 T.T. Course

This "new" motorcycle course was to lead the machines out of St. John's in the direction of Ballacraine where they effectively rejoined the Gordon Bennett route but the first real corner on the St.John's course was to prove a hazard. Approaching Ballacraine from the West the riders were faced with a ninety degree turn and even in the the first decade of the twentieth century those early machines were capable of a fair turn of speed. Many riders

33

especially the faster ones experienced difficulties at this corner. The situation was really only eased in 1910, by the provision of wooden banking. Fine if you were used to riding in a circus!

The next heart stopping moment came just a few yards up the road at the famous Ballig Bridge, now, in the last decade of the century, a very much tamed version of what it once was. Running on towards Glen Helen the course roamed through a steep sided valley, difficult to farm and almost bereft of the wooded slopes of today's course. On towards Sarah's Cottage and the rigours of Creg Willey's Hill – the riders reached the turn for Peel at Kirk Michael just at the point where the modern A4 meets the A3. Swooping down Glen Wyllin Hill the riders were moving along the Western part of the Tourist Trophy Race course in the opposite direction to the cars. Over St. Germain's level crossing – the only one on the course – there was a fast sprint into "Sunset City."

Peel was not the easiest of places to race through, particularly Church Street and Albany Road which almost amounted to a latter day version of a chicane. Once out of Albany Road, a right-angled left hander, the competitors had a clear road to Ballaleece Bridge. Over the bridge, through a left hander and the finish was in sight.

The Peel chicane. (Manx National Heritage)

By now the Islanders were starting to get used to the idea of their homeland becoming the world centre for motorsport. Road closures, barricades, ambulance stations and marshals were considered the norm, not in the least inconvenient and a small price to pay, particularly if it meant putting the Island on the map for the, by now, improving visitor arrivals. As experience of organising the racing grew so did the number of regulations governing the safety of the spectators. The appearance on the St. John's circuit for the first time ever, of printed warning notices to the public, was an historical point in the history of motorsport, marked only by a respectful acceptance on the Island that it was to everyone's benefit.

The 28th. May 1907. Lining up at the start on that historical day was a field of some nineteen competitors, comprised of thirteen single cylinder and six multi-cylinder machines. The racing was expected to be close with fierce rivalry between the singles of the Triumph and the Matchless teams. Racing over ten laps of the 15 mile 1,430 yards course would surely sort the men from the boys and machine from machine. 158 1/8th. miles later it had.

The Matchlesses of the Collier brothers were superb. Charlie won the Race with less than 3 pints of fuel to spare, brother Harry setting the lap record of 23m.5 secs, 41.81 m.p.h.. This was the start of a rivalry between the teams that was to last over the next few years on the St. John's course. However the real story lay with the Triumphs. Led home in second place by Marshall and followed in third spot by Hulbert the Triumphs had followed up their success in the London – Edinburgh 24 hour run, when fifteen out of fifteen starters had finished and had each won gold medals. The Triumphs had proved their worth under race conditions and proved in the passing, that tests of machine reliability such as the TT could provide, were right for the future of British motorcycle development.

The race for the multi-cylinder machines, the Twins, had gone well. Rem Fowler's win set the pattern for many Norton victories in the years ahead.

The results for 1907 show clear-cut victories for the first men home in each class but the races were not without excitement and their share of controversy. Excitement there was in plenty, with crashes, plug, belt and tyre changes, livestock on the course and the sheer exhaustion of the riders. Rem Fowler's spirits were at such a low ebb that he had at one point in the race almost decided to call it quits. His indomitable spirit rose quickly to the surface when a helpful spectator informed him that he was leading the second place man, W.H. "Billy" Wells by thirty minutes. All thoughts of surrender were pushed aside and the rest is as they say, "a matter for the record books."

Sarah's Cottage. Sarah Corlett and her granddaughter Maud in 1907. (Flora Callow)

Controversy reared its head in the single-cylinder race with the "experts" determining that Marshall would have won the Race if he had used pedal assistance. Well he wasn't riding a machine with pedals, therefore he couldn't use them and he lost. Obviously the judicious use of pedal power by Collier, particularly up Creg Willey's Hill, got him closest to the specified fuel consumption average. End of Controversy? Not quite. Pedals were banned from then on. The result stood. Once more the benefits of developing machinery on the Isle of Man were well proven.

Charlie Collier became the first winner of the Marquis de Mouzilly St. Mars Trophy – based on the Montagu Trophy presented to the winner of the Tourist Trophy Car Races – and £25, with Rem Fowler winning the Dr. Hele-Shaw Trophy* and £25. The 1907 results were as follows:

Single-cylinder Machines
First	C.R. Collier	Matchless	4 hrs. 8m 8 secs	38.22 m.p.h.
Second	J. Marshall	Triumph	4 hrs.19m 47 secs	37.11 m.p.h.
Third	F. Hulbert	Triumph	4 hrs.27m 50 secs	35.89 m.p.h.

Multi-cylinder Machines
First	H. Rem Fowler	Norton	4 hrs.21m 53 secs	36.22 m.p.h.
Second	W.H. Wells	Vindec	4 hrs.53m 4 secs	32.21 m.p.h.
Third	W.M. Heaton	Rex	5 hrs.11m 4 secs	28.50 m.p.h.

One experiment that was not repeated was the spraying of an acid based solution on part of the course. Designed as a means of reducing dust on the road, it had the effect of spraying man and machine, reducing the riders protective clothing to tatters and was not appreciated by wandering livestock.

The honour of providing the first foreign entries fell to Germany with two N.S.U's representing the might of the continent. This was to be no experiment; each year, as the word spread, more and more foreign entries were received, although it took almost half a century before they began to dominate the strong, ever present British.

Organisational skills were improving and the races were strengthening their reputation. Obviously there must have been collusion between the motorcycle and car organisations at various stages – the A-C.C was in fact an off-shoot of the Automobile Club – because the experience of Julian Orde and his colleagues would have been invaluable to Freddie Straight and his team. The courageous decision taken by the Auto-Cycle Club was justified.

As if there had not been enough excitement on the Island to last the year through, the next day saw the promotion of the Tourist Trophy Car Race. First run in September two years previously, this event was fast superseding the success and popularity of the Gordon Bennett Trials. Run over the 1906 course the inhabitants of St. John's, Peel and Kirk Michael needed quickly to come to terms with high speed machines coming at them from the other direction and all within a twenty four hour period. No cases of stiff necks reported there, twisted ones maybe!

Practising for the 1907 Tourist Trophy Car Race covered a period of one to two weeks dependent on whether the driver was a new entrant or not. There was speculation about the winning car; weather and road conditions might favour one car more than another. Distraction of the "competition" was a sideshow put on by drivers and mechanics and enjoyed by supporters and spectators alike. The early morning trials always had their share of "watchers" checking times and performances, which were invariably inaccurate, because of the deliberate habit of of some crews in stopping at a favourite spot for a cigarette, just to confuse the opposition and their helpers.

*The Hele-Shaw Trophy never appeared. Fifty years later Rem Fowler was presented with a substitute trophy at the TT Golden Jubilee celebrations.

The Trophy Race was to be run in conjunction with a race for Heavy cars with the entrants starting five minutes after the departure of the last Tourist car. Whilst the Tourist Trophy Race was designed as a contest for the development of the ideal touring car the Heavy cars were to compete with a windscreen – made of wood – erected behind the driver to represent the area opposing the wind of covered-in body work. The last of the windjammers!

Roads were closed from 9:00 a.m. until 6:00 p.m. allowing plenty of time for the Races. To ensure the maximum amount of fuel was available, the cars were pulled from the enclosure to the start by horse. A wet day meant that fuel consumption would increase and Wednesday 29th. May 1907 was not a good day to start with although it did clear! Thirty two cars lined up for the start of the six round marathon, the last ten away were the Heavy car contestants.

The last of the windjammers!
(Manx National Heritage)

Ten minutes after the Race started the rain did ease a little but visibility and conditions were still far from satisfactory. At 9:57 the message was passed from Ramsey that the first car was through, a Darracq driven by Algy Lee Guinness followed by the quickly moving Beeston-Humber of Reed. The news that excited the islanders was that Coatalen in the Hillman – the first Manxman entered in the Trophy Races – had passed through the Bungalow first on the road, moving from twenty fourth starting position to number one in just three-quarters of the first round. His luck broke, along with a back spring on the third round ending in retirement.

As the Races progressed more and more cars were retiring, mostly through fuel starvation and with only a couple of miles to go and one hand virtually on the Tourist Trophy, Lee Guinness's Darracq finally expired at Hilberry.

Only two cars finished in the Touring car class, the 20 h.p. Rover driven by E. Courtis taking the award after 8hrs.23m.27 secs of racing. Second car home was the Beeston-Humber of T.C Pullinger. Only two of the Heavy cars made it to the finish after their seven rounds with the G.P. Mills guided 30 h.p. Beeston-Humber being declared the winner in a time of 7hrs.11m.0 secs. In second place was Greame Feenton's Gladiator. All this on an allowance of 1 gallon per 25 miles for the tourers and 1 gallon per 16 miles for the heavies!

During the winter of 1907 a review of the regulations was undertaken by the Auto-Cycle Club and it was accepted that pedals were to be discarded, single-cylinder machines would be restricted to 100 miles per gallon and twins to 80 miles per gallon. One other notable change for 1908 was the move from May to September for both car and motorcycle races.

Competing for the second year on the St. John's course the major fear was for the weather conditions. Forecasting was not the science it is now, predictions were very much in the order of adages such as "red sky at night, sailors delight." Accustomed as they were to practising in adverse, sometimes even atrocious conditions, wet or windy weather was not conducive to improving riding skills, learning the course or indeed finding the correct settings for machines. Perhaps Mother Nature would smile kindly on them on Tuesday

22nd. September? Brilliant sunshine was the order of the day as the contenders' machines were wheeled out of the paddock. At 10:17 a.m. the first machine was dispatched to start the first of ten arduous circuits of the course.

Renewing battle from where they had left off in 1907, the Colliers were intent on showing to one and all the Matchlesses' superiority over Marshall and the Triumphs. Despite crashing on the first lap, having to stop to repair a puncture and change a broken exhaust valve, Marshall passed the early race leader Charlie Collier who had only had to deal with a plug change.

The official results showed that in the singles Race, Marshall and Collier had reversed their positions of the previous year and whilst both men averaged over 40 m.p.h. for the Race, the honour of being the first to do so fell to Marshall, who also wrested the lap record away from the Collier family. The twin-cylinder Race was won by Reed on a D.O.T., Bashall on a B.A.T. came in second and the new Belgian F.N. machine ridden by R.O. Clark hauled itself into third place. All the previous year's times for the first, second and third machines home in both classes were considerably bettered. The Belgian F.N. produced a total race time of 4 hr.11m 3 secs, one hour and one second less than Heaton's third place time in 1907.

Pure statistics make for very interesting reading but they do not tell all of the story. The TT has always been as much about people as machinery. The 1908 official results do not show for instance that the entries had risen to thirty six starters, fifteen singles and twenty one twins. Nor do the statistics show that the third man home riding a Triumph, Sir R. Arbuthnot was on special leave for the Race. This Knight of Road and Realm was also a Captain in the Royal Navy. Promoted to Admiral only a few short years after his TT success, he was, alas, lost with his ship in the Great War.

Just two days after the motorcycles had raced it was the turn of the cars. On the surface it looked as if a pattern was developing, with the cars regularly following on from the motorcycles. This, if it ever was considered as a pattern was about to come to an abrupt end. The London Times had embarked on an anti motor car racing crusade. So much fuss was created that the Automobile Club, by now granted the royal seal and called the Royal Automobile Club*, held a meeting to consider cancelling the event.

The R.A.C. decided to go ahead but to look into the most dangerous parts of the course. It was considered wise to omit the Peel town section of the course – remember the chicane effect in between Albany Road and Church Street and the ninety degree corners! Once again the regular competitors found themselves having to cope with a course change. This time the course was to go out West but then turn right at Ballacraine and rejoin the 1907 course at Kirk Michael. There was another difference in 1908 because for the first time in the brief history of car racing on the Island, a race was to start outside Douglas. Hillberry was chosen. So after all the pressures, some obvious and some not so, the scene was finally set for the 1908 Tourist Trophy Race for cars.

Entries were good. As the appointed hour drew nigh the crowds grew ever larger. A favourite spot for the spectators that day was in the garden of one particular cottage at Cronk-ny-Mona, about two hundred yards from the start. Situated on the east side of the course the site offered a good view for half a mile beyond Hillberry. Charged a shilling a time, hundreds took advantage and it was reckoned that the cottager earned enough money that day to have purchased the property. The cottage at some stage during the early adventures of the car trials and races acquired the name "Motor Car Peril," on account of some dangerous steps situated at its entrance.

*The change of title to RAC also brought about the change A-C.C. to A.C.U.

9.00 a.m. The first car, the Hutton entered by Selwyn Edge was away, but not before the driver had overcome a stall. Following at regular intervals and with varying degrees of style all cars got underway and the chase was on.

Communications around the course were primitive but nonetheless every effort was made to keep the Press informed. There was a strategically positioned blackboard upon which the "latest information" was chalked. One of the finest wielders of chalk on the Island was drafted into service, Mr. Leece, the Headmaster of St. Thomas's School.

Julian Orde had a marvellous skill with the megaphone. Throughout the long hours of the Race he kept everyone in close proximity informed of the latest details – surely one of the first commentaries in the history of motorsport.

The rounds were being clocked up and the excitement grew in proportion. From the fifth round on, the locals really had something to cheer about and to a man, woman and child were willing one particular car on to a top-three position. A Hutton driven by Watson of St. John's was going boldly where no Manxman had been before . . . the top of the leaderboard. Although first on the road from the start Watson only managed a top-three position by the end of the fifth round just 1m.11 seconds behind the second man. Could he improve with just two rounds to go? Yes! The time difference at the end of round six was down to 43 seconds.

Round seven and he is up into second place, 2m. 2 secs behind George's Darracq. Is there going to be a Manx victory? The spectators sense it.

The last round. At 3:38 p.m. the megaphone erupts with Orde informing the excited throng that Watson is past the Bungalow. The bush telegraph was really working overtime by now and all eyes were raised towards Keppel Gate. Nearly two minutes have nearly elapsed since the announcement. Pressmen, officials and spectators alike must have begun feeling that the Race was Watson's, but there was always the chance that George had slipped past the Bungalow unreported.

3:43 p.m. Thursday 24th. September 1908, we had a Manx winner! Watson crossed the line to a rapturous welcome. With the resounding cheers of the spectators ringing in his ears, he must have felt very satisfied; very satisfied indeed that his 6hrs.43m.5 3/5ths. secs of racing, at an average speed of 50 1/4 m.p.h. had brought him victory.

That evening at the Palace prize presentation, on receiving the tributes of the large crowd and his victor's laurels from Prince Francis of Teck, he and the crowd were as one as the mechanic Sharp was called to the stage to take a well deserved bow and a standing ovation.

Huttons had been built as early as 1900 in Northallerton, Yorkshire. Then followed a move to Thames Ditton, Surrey where the 1903-4-5 models were manufactured. S.F. Edge had no time for 4-cylinder engines. No cars of this type would run under the Napier banner. He was however prevailed upon to enter three special Napier manufactured 4-cylinder engined cars in the 1908 TT. Hiding them under the Hutton name Mr. Edge must have been satisfied with the result because he had been heard renouncing motor racing a day or two earlier.

During debriefing Julian Orde and his team of enthusiasts could not have been prepared for the bombshell that was about to drop on them.

The King did not like motor car racing!

The winner, Watson at "Motor Car Peril" cottage, Cronk-ny-Mona 1908. (Manx National Heritage)

In the Manx newspaper, the Mona's Herald dated the 19th. May 1909, it was reported that "the Manx Automobile Club was endeavouring to get the R.A.C to organise another road race for motors in the Isle of Man. That there was any likelihood of success is very doubtful in view of the fact that the King, who is patron of the Club, has expressed himself very strongly against road racing by motors." So there we have it, the races were disbanded.

The pioneers had run out of road. Vested interests had won the battle but not the war. The Island still had its motorcycle races, which would go on from strength to strength. Julian Orde and the Manx people could still dream of better days to come. Anyway, Kings don't last for ever, do they!

The familiar sense of excitement grew as race day approached and almost as if by way of compensation the organisers announced that in addition to the race on Thursday 23rd. September, there would be two hill climbs, at Kewaigue and from Ramsey to the Bungalow.

It was decided that the 1909 Race would have no restrictions on fuel and that engine capacity limits would be introduced instead. Single-cylinder machines were to be restricted to not more than 500 c.c. whilst twins were fixed at 750 c.c. maximum. The classes were combined and silencers done away with, but to keep faith with the "tourist concept" the regulations insisted on mudguards and saddles. The result was stereotyping of the racing and an artificial handicapping of the enterprise shown by the few makers of larger engines.

Matchless versus Triumph. The Collier brothers had decided to switch to larger engines. Easy when you own the factory. Marshall retained faith with the single-cylinder machines. That year reliability was sacrificed for speed. Fifty four starters and only nineteen finishers! Charlie Collier along with nineteen other riders failed to even reach the half-way mark. Brother Harry saved the family honour and added to the tradition of having a Collier on the rostrum by winning the race in record breaking time. Poor Marshall! After a valiant effort the Triumph suffered valve trouble and failed to finish.

In modern day racing record laps are achieved by shaving fractions of a second off here and there. It was remarkable that Harry Collier reduced 1907's fastest lap by over four minutes – 18.2%! The fifty mile an hour lap was achieved. It was no longer a dream and all this in only three years of racing. To the purist not only was the development of the motorcycle continuing apace but such ancillary matters as road surfaces must have been improving.

Chasing home in second place in a race time of 3hrs.17m.35 secs, just 3m.58 secs behind came the American G."Lee" Evans. Answering the cry "the Indians are coming," his vee-twin Indian was just a taste of what was in store a couple of years later. The Triumphs were still there enjoying success and a magnificent third place effort on the single-cylinder by Billy Newsome saw the team sharing the victor's rostrum for the third year running.

Perhaps some of the committee sensing that the challenge of the St. John's course was reaching its zenith, had already begun searching their minds for inspiration to help maintain the Island's position in the vanguard of motorcycle development. There were to be changes, but first there was the matter of the 1910 TT.

The spectacular increase in entries each year pointed to the fact that the message about the TT was getting across to the industry. The manufacturers had grasped the nettle and saw the TT for what it was, a perfect test bed for machinery and parts. Never short of ideas to promote their products and improve sales, the manufacturers and the Isle of Man Advertisement Board were delighted when the Motor Cycle magazine arranged special wire transmissions to the adjacent islands giving lap positions on the day of the Race. Situation reports were posted up in stores such as Gamages and Harrods, motorcycle agencies and depots throughout the length and breadth of the land. From Bradford, Cardiff, Dublin, Glasgow, Llandrindod Wells, and Norwich, no corner of the kingdom was untouched. This opened new avenues of opportunity to all connected with the TT and gave the Island new markets to aim at.

High speeds in the previous year caused concern for the authorities. They consequently reduced the upper engine capacity to 670 c.c. but it made little difference to the twins, as lap and race records still tumbled. To ease the way round Ballacraine corner the rough stone wall on the farm side of the road was protected by wooden banking. Sad to say, although this helped most riders, poor Harry Bowen despite setting a new race record of 53.15 m.p.h. – and it stands to this very day – came a cropper here and his race was over.

The top manufacturers met in 1910 in an atmosphere of fierce and competitive combat. The leaders were pushed hard by the B.A.T twins, with the German N.S.U.'s impressing. The international flavour of the Races was beginning to develop nicely but for the foreign machines, their time was yet to come.

First	C.R. Collier	Matchless	3 hrs. 7m 24 secs	50.63 m.p.h.
Second	H.A. Collier	Matchless	3 hrs. 12m 45 secs	48.61 m.p.h.
Third	W. Creyton	Triumph	3 hrs. 17m 58 secs	46.28 m.p.h.

Prior to race day on the 26th., there was another date in May which brought sadness to the nation but a glimmer of hope to all lovers of motorcar racing. On Friday 6th. May 1910 the announcement of the King's death was made. After a suitable period of mourning and ever hopeful that the new King might like their sport, or at the very least not make any singularly unhelpful comments, the Island began to make tentative arrangements to re-introduce car racing.

All was not doom and gloom in 1910. Indeed one of the most valuable ingredients of the TT was introduced into the mix. Scouting in the Isle of Man owed its existence to the hard work of a handful of young men. These youngsters and their leaders, some only a little older than the schoolboys in their charge, conducting themselves in a manner befitting their elders, had impressed all whose paths they crossed. In less than a handful of years since their founding, Governor Raglan had agreed to be their Patron. Under his patronage the Scout movement needed little persuasion to assist at the TT Races. This was to be no marriage of convenience as the Scouts are still there helping at the Races, some belonging to the fourth generation of families who can trace their involvement back to 1910.

No comfortable out of the way jobs for these young men. Initially they were used as signallers and posted at three hundred yard intervals all the way around the course, supplied with the now traditional whistle and flag and primed with information and skills as varied as:

Signalling in morse code (with flags) the approach of a rider.
Instructions on the removal of wreckage from the course.
Moving livestock away from the near vicinity of the race area.
First aid, crowd control and anything else that the racing authorities saw fit to throw at them.

Scouts in action in the 1910 TT.
(Manx National Heritage)

42

Later on they diversified into other fields of service, acting as messengers, flag carriers, press box attendants, scoreboard operators, number plate cleaners and so forth. Totally dedicated to the TT, there are early examples of the esteem and trust in which they were held, when they conveyed messages around the course by bicycle whilst the race was actually in progress. Many Scouts moved on to other duties as they grew older, becoming marshals, ambulancemen, policemen, firemen and riders. Some moved into administrative duties but all have one common bond, they were there in their formative years.

Across the decades there has always been acknowledgment by the riders of the part the Scouts play in the smooth running of the Races. Stanley Woods always brought a couple of boxes of toffee from Dublin to keep the boys on the scoreboards happy. Most of the victors to this day turn on the dais and reward the Scouts on the scoreboard with a glimpse of the Trophy cementing the bond the Scouts have with the TT.

Despite their long hours of duty the boys and their leaders remained ever cheerful and still do to this day, bringing great credit to the Movement, their founder, families, the Island and above all themselves.

Where else would you find a prestigious world class event having an input from accomplished youngsters in the age group 10 years and upwards? They have contributed to the TT in a magnificent manner. In the early days before public holidays they did not even volunteer, their presence was compulsory. We salute the Isle of Man Boy Scouts Movement, past, present and future.

Gaining a band of unpaid volunteers must have suited the Manx Treasury to a tee, but whilst the enthusiasm of the Scouts was infectious not everyone was pleased with the Island as a sports venue. Some people saw the races as an infringement on their personal liberty and during the pre race countdown an incident occurred which highlighted the tenuous hold the races had on all walks of Island life. True acceptance was still some way down the road.

The start area at St. John's 1910 TT. (Manx National Heritage)

1910, Tynwald Fair field. A proud Mr. Baines is standing by to inaugurate the first purpose-built scoreboards, the manning of which proved beyond the capabilities of one person. Lots of people are milling about including one or two of the local farmers who are still far from happy at this annual invasion of their territory, when one old boy Mr. Arthur Matthews of Glenmooar, intent on establishing the fact that "he still had rights" decided to prove it by trundling past in his dogcart a few minutes before the start.

He met with opposition, verbal at first, followed in very short order by physical resistance. The farmer lashed out at one young man with his whip, but the adept spectator caught the tail end and pulled the whip away from the man. The crowd cheered and closed in, so the farmer cuffed the nearest boy to hand with the pony's reins. That did it! Egged on by the crowd the boys took the pony out of its shafts and dumped the cart on the green. The air took on a particular shade of blue from the farmer's colourful language as he attempted to calm the frightened pony.

Worse followed as someone fired a cap gun and the poor beast bolted, smashing into one of the competitor's number plates. A riot was imminent. The police attempted to intervene, but not being used to large scale crowd control, and being of "a nice variety" their efforts were far from effective.

The solution was a compromise, after all that's what the British built their Empire on . . . wasn't it! Marching up to the by now semi-exhausted farmer the suggestion was made by Freddie Straight that "you seem to be a strong man, come and help us to keep order." Slapping a committee badge on the old fellow's arm, the pair of them marched off like old pals to great cheers from the crowd. Order was restored. One more convert had been made.

No requirement to convert the good burghermen of Douglas: they had known about the inherent value of the TT ever since it had started. Led by Mr. George Brown on behalf of the Douglas Jubilee Carnival Committee, strenuous efforts were made to bring car racing to the Island in the summer of 1911. After all, were not a Coronation and a Jubilee worth celebrating!

THE FOUR-INCH COURSE

The strenuous efforts made by the "Town Fathers" came to nought with the Isle of Man Highway Board declining to give permission for car racing. Perhaps their reasoning lay with the 1908 car race which had been packed full of incidents. Perhaps it lay in the knowledge that the motorcycle race organisers had aspiration to make the TT an even bigger and better event by partially utilising the Gordon Bennett course, a section of which ran through Douglas. Either way, disappointment was the result.

1911 saw the organisation of the TT handed over in its entirety to the A.C.U. Soon came a dramatic announcement that would go a long way towards lifting the mood of disappointment that prevailed on the Island. Staging the TT on the Mountain course was undoubtedly the quantum leap forward. It had effectively taken only five years for this event to grow from the status of a trailer or "B" movie, to an annual big screen hit. The announcement also brought about the first signs of commercialism of the TT.

Douglas Corporation and others set about building grandstands which occupied most of the space at what had been popular and free vantage points in Douglas during the earlier trials and car races. Public reaction to the grandstands was not favourable. Paying to watch "their races" was not part of the calculation as far as the good townsfolk were concerned. They indicated their displeasure by walking out into the countryside to find a vantage point, or they joined the large throng of people at the foot of Bray Hill.

The A.C.U. announced that there would be two races in 1911, a Junior four lap on Friday 30th June and on Monday 3rd July a five lap race for the Senior.

Virtually every manufacturer who had an genuine interest in winning the 1911 Race or at least doing well in it, on hearing of the chosen route, now directed their energies into solving the problem of getting man and machine up that eight mile climb from Ramsey to Brandywell. Not once but several times. Machines with only a single gear were not going to do well and several of the manufacturers, recognising this fact, devised various new methods of gearing to drive their machines towards the conquest of their "Everest." The Americans tackled the problem with their usual vigour devising a winning formula through two-speed gears operated by chain drive to the rear wheel.

It is fairly certain that none of the one hundred and four riders entered for those first races on the "Four inch" course – so called after the stipulation on piston length in the 1908 Car TT – could have been prepared for the challenge that lay ahead of them. That challenge drained every last ounce of energy from the riders, brought a new dimension to the meaning of stamina and tested the machines to the very uppermost limits of their capabilities. American rider Jack De Rosier was heard to comment "Tell you what boys, I guess this ain't no tea party."

Lining up for the Junior on Friday, what thoughts must have been racing through the minds of the riders. Thoughts of their own race plan, of the challenge of the mountain section, thoughts along the lines of "I hope they've remembered to open the mountain gates." Nerves had to be put to one side, all thoughts concentrated on the Race. They were off on an adventure of a lifetime.

Amongst the thirty four machines contesting the 150-mile Junior were some familiar names, Harold Collier on the single-cylinder Matchless, Percy Evans riding the twin-cylinder Humber. A hard fought race which brought eventual victory to the Humber.

"The 4-inch Course"

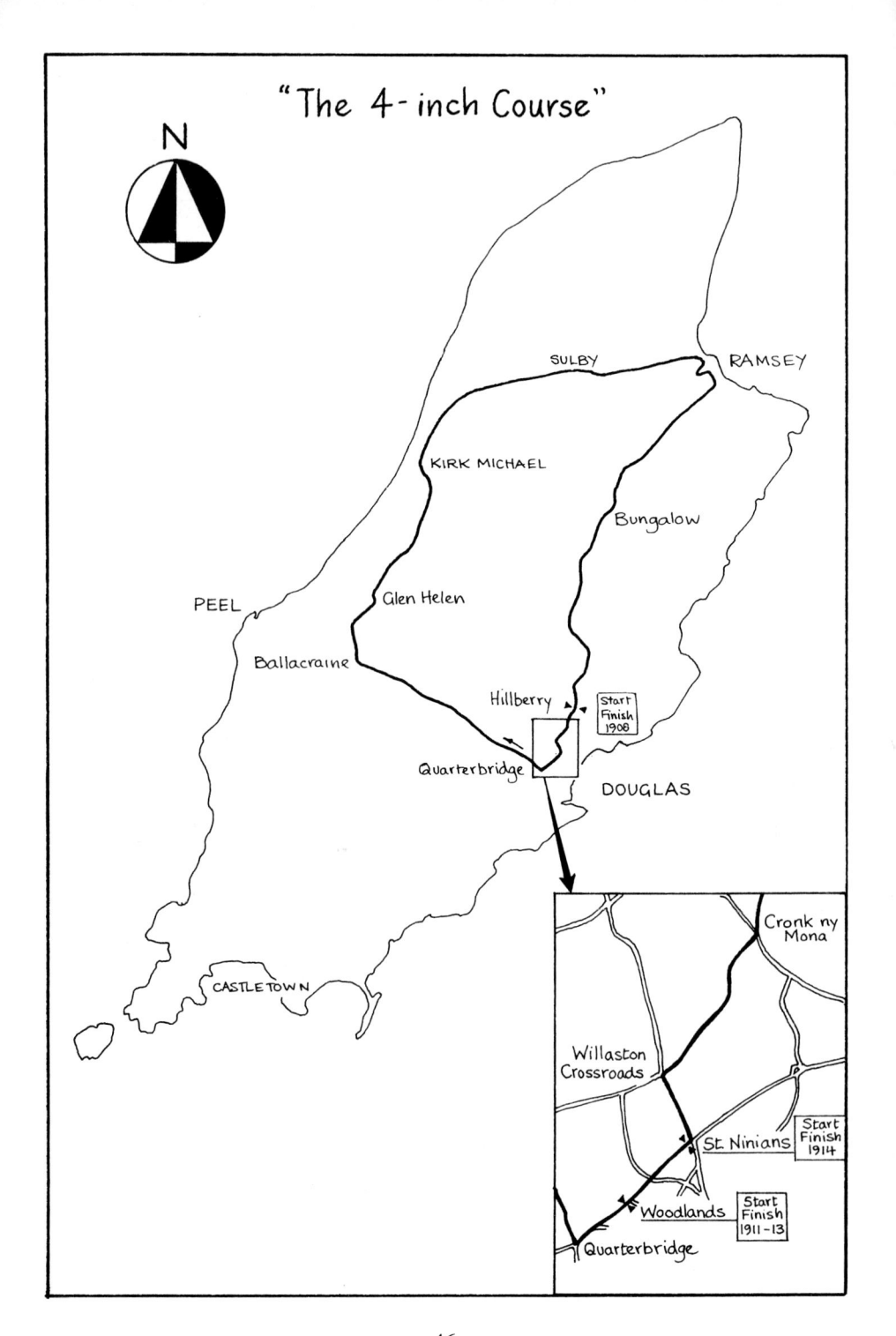

The Senior Race had everyone talking. A great wave of anticipation rolled over the Island. Anticipation of a great race and a sense of expectation that the Island was about to witness the laying of another foundation stone to the well-being of the home grown motorcycle. After all, it shouldn't take too long for the "boys" to see off the American intruders. Events were to prove otherwise and despite hard riding by Charlie Collier who forced his Matchless into second place, only to be disqualified for a non-scheduled fuel stop, nothing could prevent the race from becoming a one-two-three for the Indians. A fine effort and a damaging blow to British pride and prestige.

Winding down the activities on the 4th.July was a Flying Kilometre Race on Douglas Promenade from the bottom of Summerhill to the Palace. Ten thousand people gathered. The trial was divided into three classes; light, medium and heavy. Riders set off to cover the one kilometre of a concrete footway on the seaward side of the promenade in as short a time as possible.

Representing the U.S.A. in the heavy class, Jack de Rosier riding an Indian won. Divesting his machine of all unnecessary parts, such as mudguards and "brakes," he covered the kilometre in 29.6 seconds, a speed of 75.57 m.p.h. Apparently his face was a picture as he used his feet for brakes to avoid colliding with the large crowd of onlookers. Nice to win on American Independence Day though!

Jack De Rosier, winner of the 1911 Flying Kilometre Race.
(Manx National Heritage)

The American success of 1911 led to considerable disquiet amongst the British manufacturers. From correspondence in the motorcycle press of the day, one could be forgiven for thinking that the trans-Atlantic cousins had pulled off another Boston tea party on the unsuspecting British motorcycle industry.

Even before the A.C.U. had begun to pack for home, storm clouds were gathering and the TT was facing a challenge to its existence. Manufacturers were voicing their opinions that the course was too severe a test and threats were made to boycott the 1912 races. Complaints were lodged about the state of the roads; particular reference was made to the section down from Cronk-ny-Mona to Willaston Cross and along Ballanard Road. There had been the sad death of Victor Surridge on the Glen Helen section during practice. The safety of riders was high on the agenda. Confidence in the supremacy of British machinery had been dented. To cap it all a vociferous minority of residents led by, amongst others, the famous author Sir Hall Caine took exception to the Island being invaded by hordes of strangers who had a passion for a sport that kept the inhabitants bottled up in their homes – Hall Caine lived at Greeba Castle. The very future of the races was in jeopardy.

Somewhat battered but unbowed the 1912 TT arrived. Entries were admittedly down but with a change in the class capacity to limit the Juniors to 350 c.c. and the Seniors to 500 c.c., all looked set for a good race meeting.

Friday's Junior on the 28th. June was run in the rain. Belt-driven equipment suffered badly from loss of grip in the wet conditions. This undoubtedly gave the advantage to machines with chain-driven transmissions. Douglas machines came home in first and second place, out of a field of twenty five.

Monday's Senior heard the hills and dales echoing to the howl of the very advanced two-stroke Scotts. It might have been a one-two for them but a burst tyre at Sulby on the last lap foiled Frank Philipp and the team had to be content with Applebee's fine victory.

With two races on the "Four inch" course under their belts, the A.C.U. could begin to relax. Organising the races must have started to become easier and with the moans and groans of yesteryear dissipating, there was always the future to look forward too.

Entries for the 1913 races were a record at one hundred and forty seven. Major Tommy Loughborough took over from the brilliant Freddie Straight. He caused a "major" upset by implementing a decision to make the races even more of a test of fortitude. The Junior and Senior races were to be segmented and each part raced over two days. The Junior would have two laps on the first day and four laps run in conjunction with the second part of the Senior, a four lap race, on the second day; the first part of the Senior, a three lapper having been run earlier on, with the first part of the Junior.

This change of rule was not greeted with acclaim. It did, however, have the effect of attracting more and new manufacturers to the TT. With sixteen different makes of machine in the Junior and thirty two in the Senior there was plenty for the enthusiasts to wax lyrical about.

Before racing got underway there was the matter of the Suffragettes to clear up and clear up it was to be! There had been ugly rumours overnight on the 12th. June of "mad Suffragettes" littering the course with glass, which at one point was collected by the bucketful. The news was kept from the riders. The Vicar General took out a corps of road sweepers who stuck heroically to their brushes only finishing their task at 4:00 a.m. on the day of the Race. What an earth these women thought they could achieve was beyond the wit of the ordinary Manx person because the Island was the first place in the world to give women the vote. They recognised the publicity value of the TT as an aid to their cause.

The show had to go on. As ever the TT proved greater than any individual or group. Individual winners were Hugh Mason on a NUT in the Junior and a Scott ridden by Wood brought them honour and glory in the Senior for the second consecutive year with the new manufacturer's prize being taken by Rover.

The biggest problem that was to occupy the manufacturers that close season involved tyres. Many machines had suffered from tyres creeping and covers blowing off rims. Arguments there were in plenty about the ever rising speeds particularly from the 3-1/2 h.p. machines. Some people thought they were too fast for the twisty course and there was talk of reducing engine capacity again and even discussion on the re-introduction of fuel consumption measures. All these ideas were put to one side on the grounds that sales would be adversely affected. One successful footnote to the races was the use of fishnets on which metal letters and numbers were fastened and hung across the road at certain critical points indicating distances from corners; an improvement on the earlier painted canvasses and the forerunners of the very efficient modern day race signposting.

More changes were afoot for the 1914 Tourist Trophy Races. Once again the start was on the move because more paddock space was required. This time the chosen site was the top of Bray Hill, affording the riders every opportunity of overcoming any reluctance on the part of the machine to cough into life. The finishing line was at the end of Ballanard Road at its junction with Bray Hill. This decision was to have an unforeseen and tragic sequel.

The Junior race on Tuesday 19th. May was won despite atrocious conditions by the A.J.S.'s Eric Williams in first place and Cyril Williams second 4m.44 secs. behind. The first and second place men were still congratulating each other when word arrived of a most terrible accident. Frank Walker on a Royal Enfield had been leading on the second lap when a spill handed the lead to the two A.J.S.'s. Remounting he chased after the two Williams with such determination that twice more man and machine parted company. Approaching the finish at speed he claimed third place as he flashed over the finish line.

In choosing the finish line position the organisers had made allowances for a slowing up area by utilising the first one hundred yards or so of Ballaquayle Road. Poor Frank was travelling at such speed that in the space of what must have seemed like a split second to a man who would be near exhaustion, never mind any possible injuries, was confronted by an excited crowd of spectators. Normally it would have been possible for a rider to pull up in time, but this was no ordinary set of circumstances and in a final brave effort to avoid injuring any spectator he turned the machine down into Laureston Road (now the start of Woodbourne Road) and met an untimely end in a collision with a heavy wooden barrier. This tragic accident brought into widespread use the rope barriers as we know them today. There could hardly have been a dry eye in the Island that day and such is the still the effect on every Island home whenever one of the "boys" is injured or worse.

The Senior on Thursday 21st. must have been a fantastic race with only 6m.24 secs separating the first three men home and that after over four hours of effort. This was also the first dead heat in the history of the TT with H.R. Davies on his Sunbeam being credited with the same time – 4hr.39m.12 secs. – as O.C. Godfrey on the Indian, behind the winner C.G. Pullin on a Rudge.

Godfrey's team-mate Paul Derkum must surely have been in line to collect a prize for the furthest travelled rider that year. Crossing the Atlantic in the Mauretania he was marconigrammed two days out of Liverpool to make sure he had his baggage ready for immediate disembarkation on arrival. Thirty minutes after the Cunarder had tied up, he sailed from the Mersey bound for Douglas and his first practice session.

After a lapse of five years during which the cars had been sorely missed, Ellan Vannin stood ready to greet the entrants and supporters to the longest race ever to be held in this fair isle. Road surfaces on the Island had improved somewhat since 1908. Each year strenuous efforts were made to subdue the dust lying on the circuit but the sheer logistics of treating the entire course were beyond the resources of the authorities.

The turning point came in 1914, when large supplies of Akonia were obtained and the Snaefell mountain road was treated for the first time. But that was of academic interest. All the 1914 competitors and manufacturers wanted to do was to test man and machine against the "Four-inch" circuit.

A test it was to be with a total of sixteen rounds to be raced over two days. Six hundred miles of hard driving lay ahead and such was the perceived prestige of the race that "The Daily Telegraph" presented a considerable sum of money to the RAC to be divided up as prize money. The winner would pick up a handsome £1,000 and the Tourist Trophy, reputed to be worth £1,000. Second car home would be awarded £250 with a special prize of £100 for the best performance by a car using a fuel other than one that was exclusively petrol. There was also a team prize of £300.

In addition, a trophy was to be awarded to the driver whose car made the best aggregate time during the sixteen ascents of the mountain section between Ramsey and the Bungalow. This trophy known as the "Henry Edmunds Challenge Trophy" had been in existence since 1902 and was in the form of a 1902 racing motor car. Designed and executed in bronze by the Viennese sculptor Gustav Gurschner, its current holder, Mr. Richard Lisle, would be trying hard in his Star to repeat his success from the last time it was competed for in 1910.

Considering that the first prize for winning the Senior motorcycle TT in 1914 was £50 it seemed that the two wheeled boys were only the poor relations, but the passage of time was to prove where the true spirit of racing lay.

A marathon race of this nature required very careful stewarding, so the course was divided into eighteen sections each in the charge of a highly respected person, many of them drawn from the ranks of the Manx Automobile Club*. Ambulance units, stretcher parties and medical practitioners were stationed right around the course. Each section steward was to keep the secretary of the meeting fully informed and the stewards in charge of the club enclosure, the paddock at Parkfield, had complete control over all matters during the racing. An early version of the Clerk of the Course perhaps!

All the competing cars were of the four-cylinder variety and were the fastest ever seen on the Island, with speeds of over 95 m.p.h. being recorded on certain parts of the course during the two weeks of the practices. Speed was one thing, reliability over sixteen laps and two days was another. Julian Orde, still there proving his worth and his intrinsic value to the Isle of Man must have felt some disappointment that only six cars out of twenty two starters completed the Race.

*The Manx Automobile Club was founded on the 20th March 1905.

During the night until half an hour before the start on Wednesday 15th. June rain had fallen making for heavy going. In sunshine and promptly at 9:00 a.m. the first car, a yellow painted Minerva driven by J. Pororato was dispatched on its marathon journey. A journey that would see him finish in fifth place and win with his colleagues – in second and third places – the team prize. Following Pororato at ninety second intervals were some famous racing names and with their brightly painted cars a kaleidoscope of racing was assured.

The Bray Hill start of the 1914 Car Race.
(Manx National Heritage)

At the end of the first day's racing the Lee Guinness brothers were in first and second place with a mere 3m.10 secs. separating them and in third position Pororato 12m.12 secs behind, in a half-way race time of 5 hrs.31m 9 secs.

Word spread around the Island that Wednesday's racing had been magnificent and with Thursday's ideal weather conditions, even bigger crowds secured vantage points about the course. The Douglas shopkeepers proclaimed a holiday which helped swell the crowds even more so. The competitors were in good spirits and a second day of excellent racing was anticipated. Indeed the grandstand at the start was virtually full before the first car was flagged away at 9:00 a.m..

K. Lee Guinness in his Sunbeam led the second day's thirteen starters all the way home, chased by his brother "Algy" until his breakdown on the thirteenth round, disappointing all those who had hoped for a Sunbeam one – two.

Winning the Race at an average speed of 56.44 m.p.h. in a total time of 10hrs. 37m 49 secs this TT giant also won the "Henry Edmunds" Trophy with an aggregate time of 1hr.56m 46 secs, a good 8m.37 secs better than the next best competitor Riecken in a Minerva, who had also claimed second spot overall 19m.49 secs behind Lee Guinness. The climbing ability of the Sunbeam over the mountain section accounted for almost half the winning margin.

51

In the concluding speeches at the Palace that evening, tribute was paid to the far sighted policies of the Manx Government and the tremendous support of the Manx Nation. The grateful thanks of the motor car industry were passed on to the Island.

As the storm clouds had gathered in 1911 so they were to gather again in 1914, this time for entirely different reasons. Just fifty five days after the 1914 event had ended and agreement for the 1915 races had been drawn up, the First World war erupted. It may be some small comfort that the years of machine development witnessed on this peaceful Island were to be put to good use in the less than pleasant atmosphere of the battlefield.

THE MOUNTAIN CIRCUIT (6)

With the Empire having been occupied in other matters the re-start of the TT on Tuesday 15th. June 1920 was eagerly awaited. Supporters of the event could be forgiven for believing that trouble and strife was well behind them. Not so!

The British Government was giving serious consideration to the imposition of Petrol Duty. A member of Tynwald, one Hugo Teare M.H.K., was earnestly seeking monetary gain from renting out his own private portion of the TT course. The Isle of Man Steam Packet was trying to replace its war losses, not an easy task, for Britain was exhausted and desperately short of materials after five long years of war. On the A.C.U. front a decision had been taken once again to move the start and finish area and they had stipulated a minimum field for each race, of thirty machines.

A key decision was also taken to switch the route away from the "Four-inch" course. This involved the course going directly on from Cronk-ny-Mona to Signpost Corner, where it turned right, through an almost ninety degree angle before carrying on to the left hander at Bedstead Corner. Once round Bedstead there is a short straight then the twisty section between the Nook and Governor's Bridge to negotiate, out of the dip and the finish is in sight.

A number of the problems were quickly overcome; the British Government did not impose Petrol Duty, the Steam Packet embarked upon a swift fleet replacement programme in time to bring the supporters and spectators over for the races. Thirty one machines started in the Senior and although the new Lightweight class was amalgamated into the Junior, entries failed to reach the stipulated requirement but racing went ahead. One problem still remained – what to do about the Hugo Teare situation!

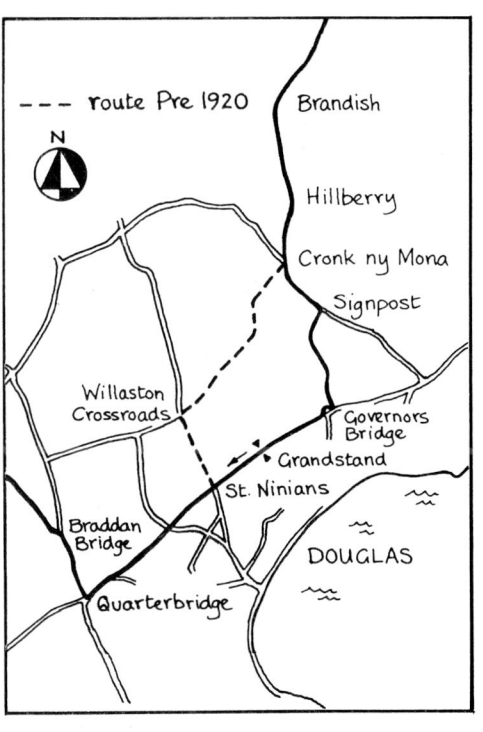

Way back in 1904 during the Julian Orde survey, the inspection party came upon Queen's Pier Road, Ramsey. A length of Queen's Pier Road from approximately the site of the current Bus Station to what is now called Cruikshanks Corner lay in private ownership. On discovering this fact Mr. Orde and his small team sought out the owner Mr. Cruikshank and asked his permission to include his private driveway as part of the Gordon Bennett course. Permission to do so was readily and graciously granted by this gentleman, who served this Island so well for many years as High Bailiff for Ramsey and Peel. Racing by cars and motorcycles continued on his driveway uninterrupted from 1904 until 1908 and between 1911 to 1914 when the Great War intervened. It was not the best of roadways and motorcyclists had often to revert to riding along the footpaths for easier progress, but at least it was there and free.

53

Mr. Cruikshank passed on in 1916 and after a short period of ownership by a family of Scots, it came Hugo Teare's way in 1919. On the revival of racing in 1920, an assumption was naturally made by the A.C.U. that the course could continue as normal out of Ramsey to the Hairpin via May Hill and Cruikshanks Corner. Not so, indicated our less than friendly politician, as he metaphorically held his hand out ... he wanted a handsome cash payment for the use of his driveway!

High Bailiff Cruikshank.
(Manx National Heritage)

There was a stand off for two years, during which time the course detoured out of Parliament Square via Albert Road and Tower Road before passing the front entrance of Teare's home "Cronk Brae" and back onto the old route. Hansard reports that in Tynwald on the 5th. May 1922, Hugo Teare was on his feet asking the Highway Board if they had an answer to the private roadway situation in Queen's Pier Road. The solution reached was a very private one between the Authorities and Teare – Ramsey Town Commissioners' engineers repaired the road surface and the A.C.U. paid the bill. Racing resumed on that particular stretch of road and Tuesday 30th. May 1922 marks the first day that the Mountain Circuit as it is today was first raced upon.

Back to the 1920 races and results. The Junior 350 c.c. was a race of heroic proportions. Eric and Cyril Williams (not related) turned out on the A.J.S. machines determined to repeat their performances of the 1914 Junior. Eric set the lap record for the course but failed to finish. This left the way open for Cyril to go one better than his 1914 second place. He did it, but only by coasting and pushing in from Keppel Gate. After over four and a half hours and 187-1/2 miles of racing, his winning margin of 9m.10 secs. when seen as the written word, conceals a picture of true devotion to the sport, the manufacturer and the spectators. Watson-Bourne second and Holroyd third, both mounted on Blackburnes completed the triumvirate. The last man home Jack Thomas, did not start until 9:54 a.m. and owing to a variety of troubles only finished at 3:47 p.m., truly a marathon race when you consider that he was at the start before 9:00 a.m.

The Lightweight 250 c.c. Junior was a walk over for the Levis stable with the first three spots filled by their machines. R.O. Clark finished exactly eight minutes behind the third placed Holroyd in the 350's, thus winning the 250 and might have snatched first place overall if he had not fallen off just before Keppel Gate, causing him to limp home the last few miles of the Race.

The popular Tommy De La Hay won the Senior at an average speed of 51.48 m.p.h. taking 4hr.22m.23 secs. to cover the 226.5 miles of the mountain circuit. Following the Sunbeam across the line* 3m.52 secs. later came Manxman Douggie Brown on a Norton. This was Douggie's best finish in all races since 1910, although he had won a trophy as a member of the Rover team in 1913. Setting the record lap on the course was a newcomer to Isle of Man racing George Dance, who before he retired with engine trouble completed a lap at a speed of 55.62 m.p.h for the 37-3/4 miles. Reg Brown got on a finishers' podium twice in 1920 with a win in the Manx Gold Cup on a borrowed horse at Belle Vue, to add to his well earned third place in the Senior.

Ever open to ideas for improving the race meeting, the A.C.U. greeted a suggestion in 1920, that sidecar racing should be introduced in the 1921 TT with mild interest; comments in the press were vehemently opposed to the idea. The manufacturers were not at all enthusiastic and the sidecars had to wait until 1923 for their turn. The Dunlop Tyre company came up trumps in '21 by supplying a good number of flagmen to assist in the marshalling.

Gold medals appeared on the prize list for 1921, being added to the £50 – £25 – £15 monetary rewards for the first three riders home in the Senior: the fastest team of three riders finishing within thirty minutes of the winner's time would be awarded individual gold medals. Viewed in the light of current rewards for sporting prowess, particularly in non-motorcycle activities, the prizes now look like small change, but remember a top of the range Indian solo machine cost £181-14s-0d in 1920.

The return, in significant numbers of the works teams boosted the total entries in 1921 to a grand total of 133 riders and machines. Amongst the thousands of spectators who flocked to the Island that year was a young man who fell instantly in love with Manxland and the TT. Watching the Senior from Hillberry he was captivated by the thrill of it all and with the single-minded sense of purpose that became his hall-mark, set about planning his return as a competitor for the next year's races. The keen young man's name ... Stanley Woods, and the rest as they say, really was history!

*The start/finish line, scoreboard and grandstand in 1920 were approximately 200 yards closer to Bray Hill than they are at present.

It was to be a good race meeting for the A.J.S. camp, with H.R."Howard" Davies coming second in the Junior 350 c.c. class splitting his team mates Eric Williams – having better luck than in 1920 – and Manxman Tom Sheard in third place. Three different machines featured in the top three positions at the end of the 250 c.c. Race with Doug Prentice on a New Imperial a convincing victor ahead of G.S. Davison's Levis and third place man W.G. Harrison on board a Velocette. A red letter day for the New Imperial and Velocette with a first appearance for both on the dais.

What a Race the Senior was to produce two days later on Thursday 16th. June, with Howard Davies winning the blue riband event on his 350 A.J.S. Foiled by a puncture from claiming victory in the Junior he planted his name firmly in the record books with the one and only win by a Junior machine in the Senior TT. Freddie Dixon used this Race to establish himself as a regular in the winner's enclosure, riding his Indian into second place a commendable 2m.13 secs behind the total race time of 4hrs.9m 22 secs of "H.R.D." H. Le Vack rounded off a good Senior for the Indians, finishing 31 secs. behind his colleague.

Preparations for the 1922 Races were disrupted by a bitter dispute over the cost of running the TT. The A.C.U. compounded this by considering invitations to hold the TT in either Yorkshire or Belgium. There were also fears for riders' safety with the approach of the 60 m.p.h.lap – it was almost achieved by Alec Bennett in the Senior of that year when he posted a new record lap of 59.99 m.p.h. In the end common sense prevailed and diplomacy won, but there was also a suspicion that only the Isle of Man could really deliver the goods.

Amongst many pre-race utterances from the A.C.U. in 1922 was an announcement that agreement had been reached with the Chief Constable of Liverpool to provide special traffic arrangements for motorcyclists crossing to the Isle of man for the TT; he promised no delays or hindrance. Garages in Liverpool also began providing parking facilities for the fans' machines at 9d. per night for solos, 1s/3d per night for sidecar combinations.

An extra Race was effectively introduced on the first Race day of 1922, Tuesday 30th. May, by splitting the 250 c.c. machines away from, but run simultaneously with the 350 c.c.'s

Setting out in the 350 at number 44 – the Lightweights were numbered 1-33 and went first – Manxman Tom Sheard on his A.J.S. carried the hopes of the Island with him. The nation was not to be disappointed and Tom Sheard, although no one realised it at the time, became the first man to complete the distance and the first to win a TT Race on the "New Mountain Course" as we now know it, and in doing so became the first Manx winner of a TT.

Clocking a time of 3hr.26m.38 secs. at an average speed of 54.75 m.p.h. was no mean feat especially as he finished 11m. 39 secs. ahead of team mate Grinton. Making his debut as he had promised was seventeen year old Stanley Woods. This greatest of riders finished fifth on his Cotton despite having the machine on fire at a pit stop and completing the race without brakes.

Geoff Davison won the 250 Race on the Levis in a time of 3hrs.46m 56 secs, a time 32 secs. faster than Jack Thomas's third place in the 350 on the Sheffield Henderson. A popular win for this famous journalist; but setting his stall out for the future was eighteen year old Walter Handley. Although he failed to finish, Handley set a lap record at 51.00 m.p.h. almost 5 m.p.h. faster than the previous year's record breaking 250 lap.

Thursday 1st June was to be Alec Bennett's day. His Sunbeam performed superbly and he won the Senior Race after leading the field from start to finish – another first for the "new course" and the TT – finishing the 226.5 miles in 3hrs.53m 2 secs. Walter Brandish stamped his name indelibly on the course in 1923 – the first rider to have a bend named after him; but in 1922 he had to make do with second place and in the process failed by a mere 22 seconds to emulate Bennett's feat of breaking the 4 hours for the distance.

The Scotts were out in force in the Senior and H. Langman furnished the team with a good individual effort by claiming third place. Not so fortunate was one Jimmy Simpson. Jimmy's introduction to the Island began in the 1922 Senior but a split tank on the Scott brought retirement on the first lap, although he had already shown enough talent to mark him down as a future star. Jimmy recorded eight fastest laps in his time. His legacy is the Jimmy Simpson Trophy for the fastest lap of the meeting.

The exit from Ramsey – White Gates in the 1920's.
(Manx National Heritage)

So there we have it! After eighteen years of racing by cars and motorcycles the Island had a permanent home for the TT, a venue that would serve motorsport well for more than another eight decades. Only one more bit of history making remained for that golden year. On Thursday 22nd. June, three weeks after the TT Races, motor car racing was resurrected.

Disappointment was probably the by-word for the 1922 Car TT. Disappointment that the entries were few and that some drivers of international repute felt the need to be elsewhere, was not going to be sufficient an excuse to prevent the organising committee from putting on a good show.

Nine cars started in the Junior Race, which was for machines of less than 1500 c.c. (the Senior was for 3000 c.c.cars). K. Lee Guinness, the last winner of the Tourist Trophy had to scratch at the last moment with terminal clutch trouble but brother Algy was there to represent the family. Powerful names lined up for the start of the six lap race. The first four laps were very close with the lead being alternately shared between Lee Guinness and Albert Divo. Not until the fourth lap did a significant gap appear and by then Sir Algy Lee

Guinness was on his way to victory. The winning Talbot-Darracq's time of 4hr.14m.56 secs. was 2m.42 secs. ahead of Divo's Talbot-Darracq. A respectable third place was achieved by Maury's Crossley-Bugatti – a French car that would soon after be manufactured in Manchester.

It would be difficult with only eight cars entered in the International Tourist Trophy Race – they actually referred to it as the Senior Race that year – to predict a likely winner, particularly as the weather was far from promising. Conditions on the course were terrible resulting in the cars posting times that were slower than the motorcycles. The Bentley stable had a good race with 2nd.-4th.-5th. places split only by Payne's Vauxhall. Home in first place after a testing eight laps came Chassagne driving a Sunbeam 3-litre straight-8 at an average speed of 55.78 m.p.h. a race time of 5hrs.24m 50 secs; compare that with the winning average speed of Bennett three weeks earlier! Sunbeam were not worrying about times. They had done the double.

It seems ironic that the French who reigned supreme at the start of the century should be present at what turned out to be the one and only car race around the "New Mountain Course". Attending this farewell party was that great and good friend of the Isle of Man, the newly knighted Sir Julian Orde. What a record he had and what pride the Island can take in the part it has played in the development of the automobile. As we know, it was not the end of car racing on the Island and the TT has gone on from strength to strength.

The authors have told the story of the early years of course development and racing on the Island, but it is not just a story of riders and machines; it is a record of dedication by ordinary people, men, women and children, young and old, the unsung heroes who make it all happen . . . . a love affair without end.

As Steve Hislop says **"You couldn't do it now!"**

HISLOP: HIS LAP

The Isle of Man TT course is the most demanding road racing circuit in the world. Every inch of its 37 3/4 miles has to be memorised and even when you know it as well as I do six laps of high speed racing requires total concentration.

I enjoy the challenge of the TT and to help you enjoy the thrills of this famous event, my colleagues and I have designed a new map of the course which we hope will give you an insight into the demands made of man and machine.

On the following pages we show a profile of the course. The road is contoured featuring the backdrop of scenery as viewed from outside the circuit and because the TT runs in a clockwise direction these pages are read from right to left.

Once past the contoured section it's time to mount up and try a lap from the comfort of your armchair or your favourite vantage point. The course is shown as a series of maps based on my film, 'T.T. Flyer' . . . but remember the speeds indicated were achieved under racing conditions, on closed roads. Please don't try to emulate your heroes.

There are visual references to famous vantage spots on each map page and these are supported by an index of place names. Additionally we have indicated various facilities around the course and a key to vantage points.

Don't forget many of the viewing positions are on private land so please treat everywhere with respect. Please take your litter to an appropriate place – rubbish blowing about the course definitely does not help.

The Police and marshals are there to help us all have a good race and watch out for special notices, particularly public warning notices.

Motorcycling is a dangerous sport.

Enjoy the maps and I hope it helps you to enjoy the racing even more.

Steve.

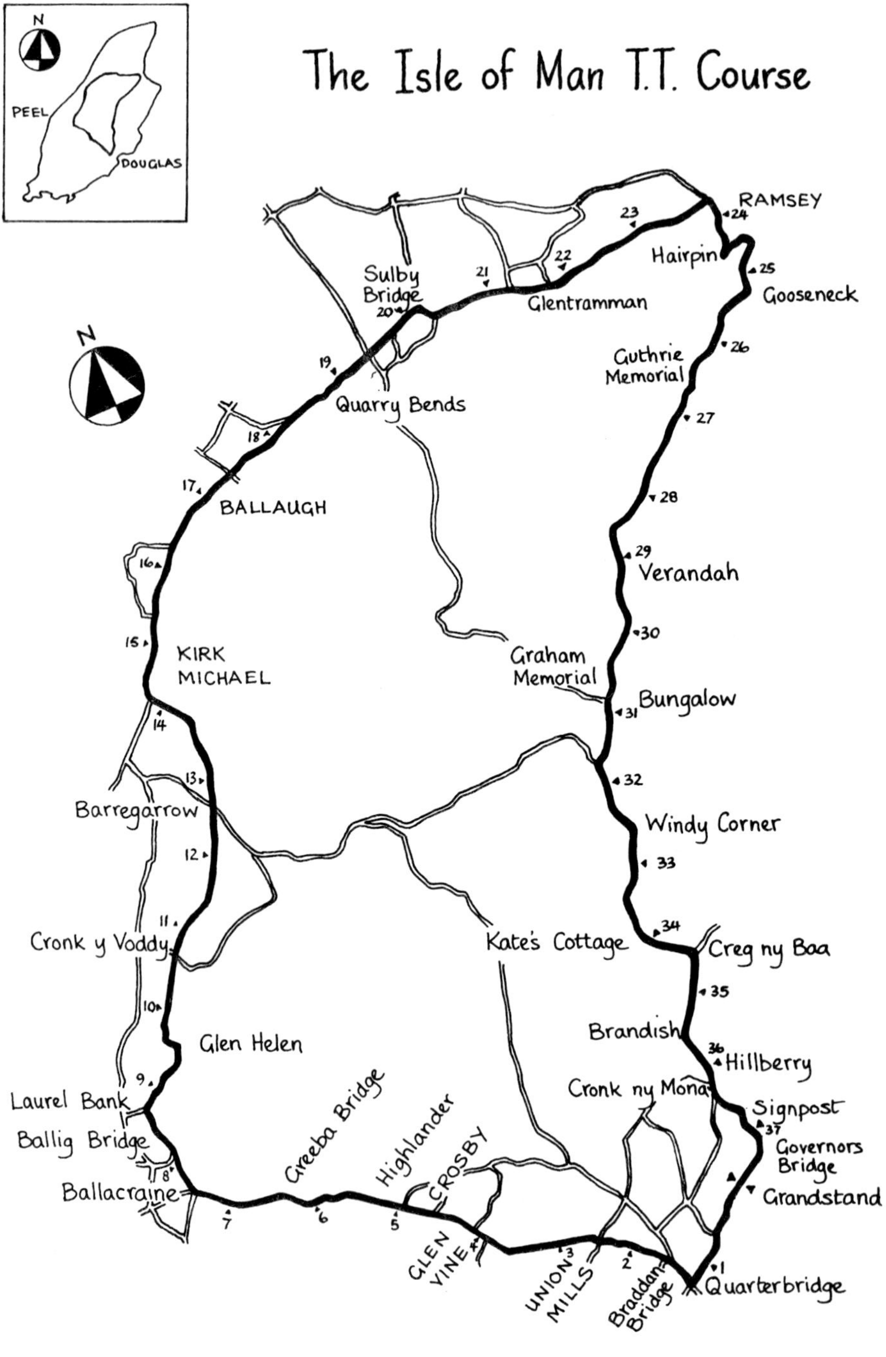
The Isle of Man T.T. Course
N
PEEL
DOUGLAS
N
RAMSEY
Hairpin
Gooseneck
Glentramman
Sulby Bridge
Quarry Bends
Guthrie Memorial
BALLAUGH
Verandah
KIRK MICHAEL
Graham Memorial
Bungalow
Windy Corner
Barregarrow
Cronk y Voddy
Kate's Cottage
Creg ny Baa
Brandish
Glen Helen
Hillberry
Cronk ny Mona
Laurel Bank
Signpost
Ballig Bridge
Governors Bridge
Creeba Bridge
Highlander
CROSBY
Grandstand
Ballacraine
GLEN VINE
UNION MILLS
Braddan Bridge
Quarterbridge

KEY

L = Locked in. You may not move from here until "Roads Open" car has passed and you are instructed to do so by a marshal.

T = Toilets.

F = Food.

D = Drinks.

* = Reasonable view.

** = Good view.

*** = Very good view.

**** = Excellent view.

***** = Brilliant view.

There are many places in the Isle of Man with the same name. All the names referred to in this index relate to the TT Course. The authors would be grateful for any information from readers on place names from the past which they may have inadvertently omitted.

INDEX

Ago's leap	71	Crosby Hotel	73
Alpine Cottage	81	Cruikshanks	87
Appledene	75	Cutting (The)	87, 93
Ballacraine	75	Doran's Bend	75
Ballacrye	81	Douglas Road Corner	79
Ballafreer	73	Drinkwater's Bend	77
Ballagarey	73		
Ballagarraghyn	75	East Mountain Gate	89
Ballahutchin Hill	73	Eleventh Milestone	77
Ballakillingan	85	Erinville	79
Ballaspur	75		
Ballaugh Bridge	81	George's Folly	89
Ballavagher	73	Ginger Hall	83
Ballavitchel Lane	73	Glen Darragh Road	73
Ballig Bridge	75	Glen Duff	85
Barregarrow	79	Glen Helen	77
Barregarrow Crossroads	79	Glenlough	73
Bedstead Corner	95	Glen Moar Mills	75
Birkin's Bend	81	Glentramman	85
Bishopscourt	81	Glen Vine	73
Black Dub	77	Gob-ny-Geay	93
Black Hut	89	Gob y Volley	83
Bottom of Barregarrow	79	Gooseneck	87
Braddan Bridge	71	Gorselea	75
Brandish	93	Governor's Bridge	95
Brandywell	91	Graham Memorial	91
Bray Hill	71	Grandstand	71, 95
Bridge (The)	87	Greeba Bridge	75
Bungalow	91	Greeba Castle	75
Bungalow Bridge	91	Greeba Young Men's Hall	75
		Guthrie Memorial	87
Church Hall Corner	73	Gwen's	81
Churchtown	85		
Coan Buigh	81	Hailwood Height	91
Creg Willey's Hill	77	Hailwood Rise	91
Creg-ny-Baa	93	Hairpin (The)	87
Cronk Breck	75	Half-way Post	83
Cronk-ny-Mona (Shelter)	93	Handley's Corner	77
Cronk Urleigh	79	Hawthorn	75
Cronk-y-Voddy	77	Highlander	73
Crosby Crossroads	73	Hillberry	93

62

INDEX

Kate's Cottage	93	Selborne Drive	71
Keppel Gate	93	Signpost Corner	95
Keppel Hotel	93	Snugborough	71
Kerrowmoar	83	Stella Maris	87
		Stonebreaker's Hut	89
Lambfell	77	Strang Road	71
Lambfell Beg	77	Sulby Bridge	83
Lambfell Moar	77	Sulby Crossroads	83
Laurel Bank	75	Sulby Straight	83
Lezayre	85		
		Thirteenth Milestone	79
Manx Motor Museum	73	Thirty Second Milestone	91
Marown Church	73	Threequarter-way Post	89
May Hill	87	Tower Bends	87
Milntown	85	Trollaby Lane	71
Mitre Hotel	79	TT Grandstand	71, 95
Mountain Box	89	Thirty Third Milestone	91
Mountain Mile	89	Top of Barregarrow	79
Murray's Motor Museum	91	Twenty Sixth Milestone	87
Ninth Milestone	75	Union Mills	71
Nook (The)	95		
		Verandah (The)	89
Orrisdale	81		
		Waggon and Horses	73
Parkfield (Corner)	71	Waterworks (The)	87
Parliament Square	85	Westwood	79
Pear Tree Cottage	73	White Gates	87
Pinfold Cottage	85	Wild Life Park	83
		Windy Corner	91
Quarry Bends	83		
Quarterbridge	71		
Quarter-way Post	77		
Ramsey Bus Station	85		
Ramsey Hairpin	87		
Raymotors	85		
Rhencullen	81		
St. Ninian's	71		
Sarah's Cottage	77		
School House Corner	85		

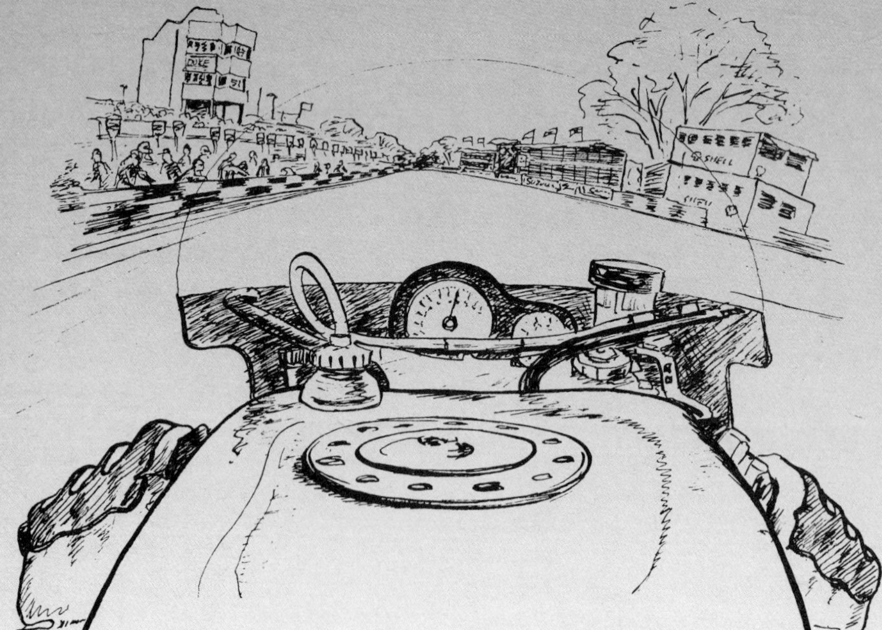
DUKE
SHELL

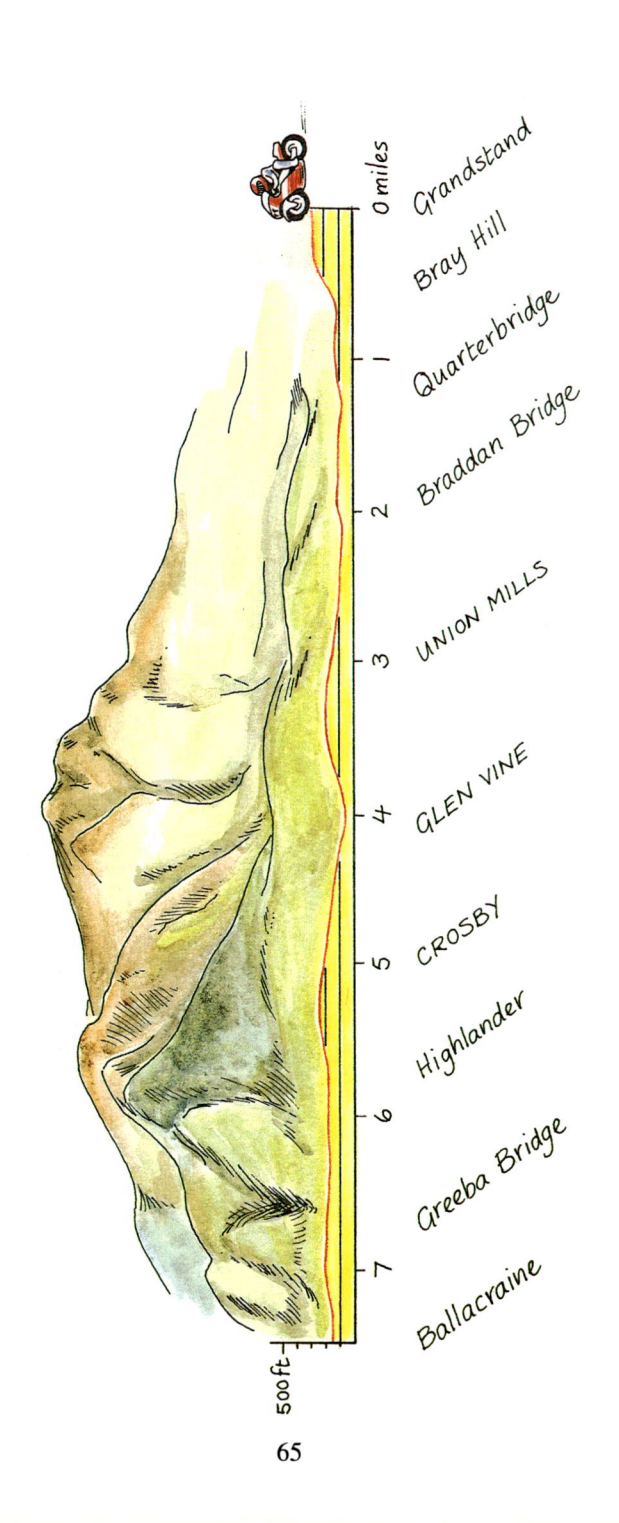

Miles	Location
0	Grandstand
	Bray Hill
1	Quarterbridge
2	Braddan Bridge
3	UNION MILLS
4	GLEN VINE
5	CROSBY
6	Highlander
	Greeba Bridge
7	Ballacraine

500ft

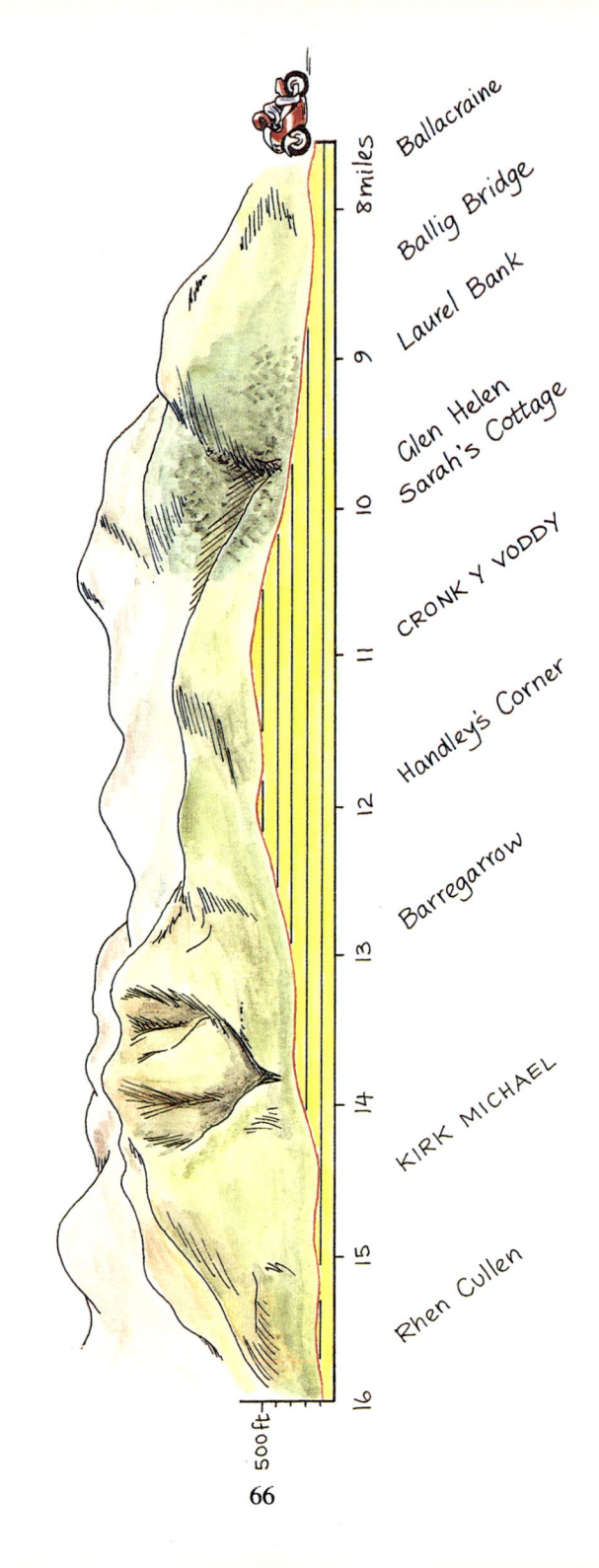

Miles	Location
8	Ballacraine
	Ballig Bridge
	Laurel Bank
9	
	Glen Helen
10	Sarah's Cottage
11	CRONK Y VODDY
12	Handley's Corner
13	Barregarrow
14	KIRK MICHAEL
15	Rhen Cullen
16	

500ft

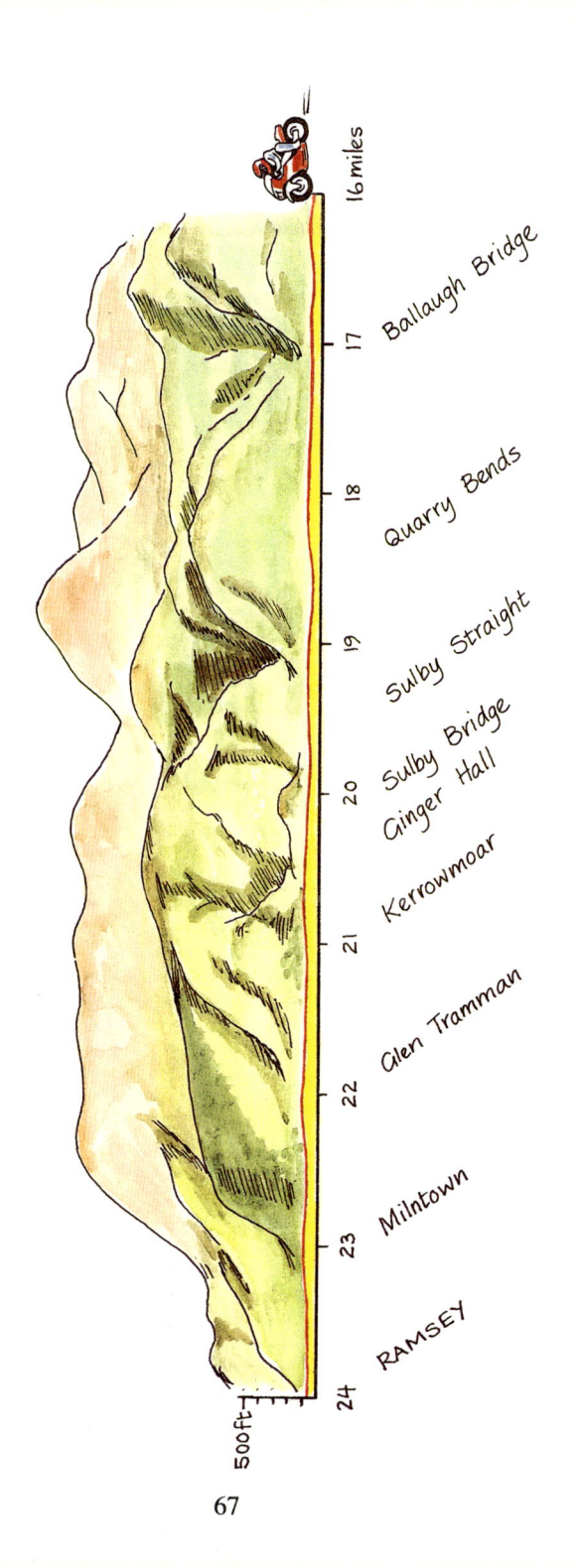

16 miles
17 Ballaugh Bridge
18 Quarry Bends
19 Sulby Straight
20 Sulby Bridge
Ginger Hall
21 Kerrowmoar
22 Glen Tramman
23 Milntown
24 RAMSEY

500 Ft

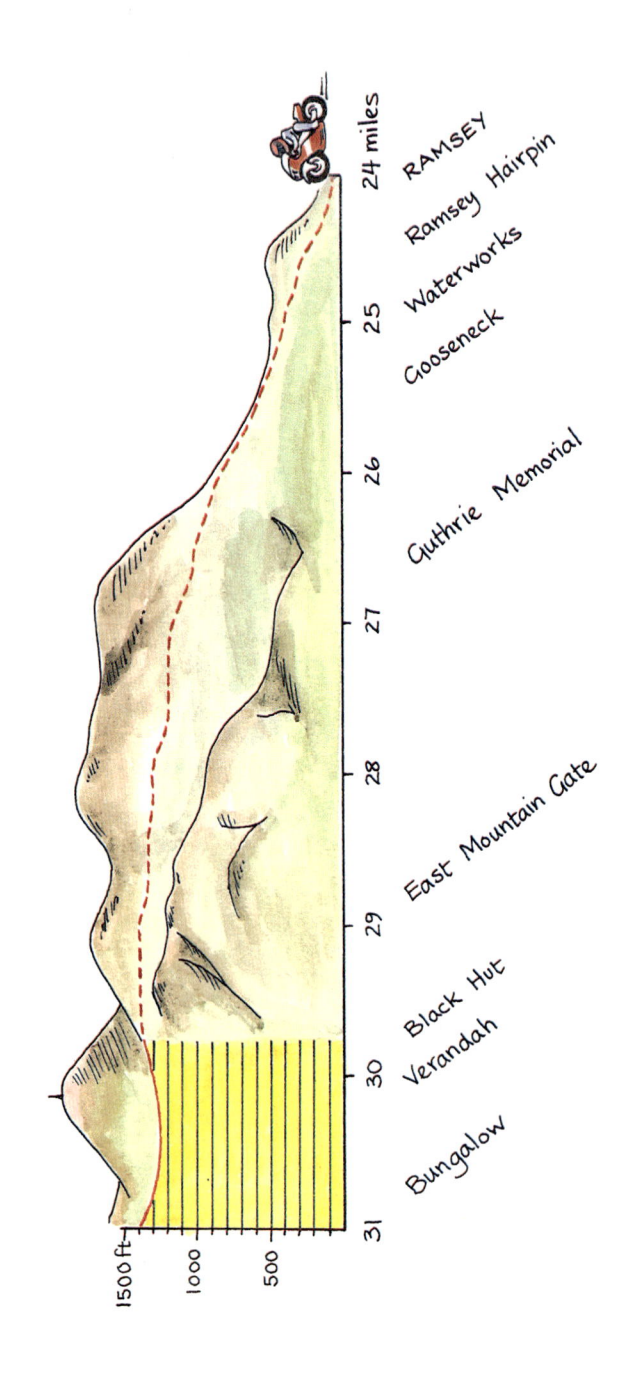

24 miles — RAMSEY
Ramsey Hairpin
25 — Waterworks
Gooseneck
26 — Guthrie Memorial
27
28 — East Mountain Gate
29
Black Hut
30 — Verandah
Bungalow
31

1500 ft
1000
500

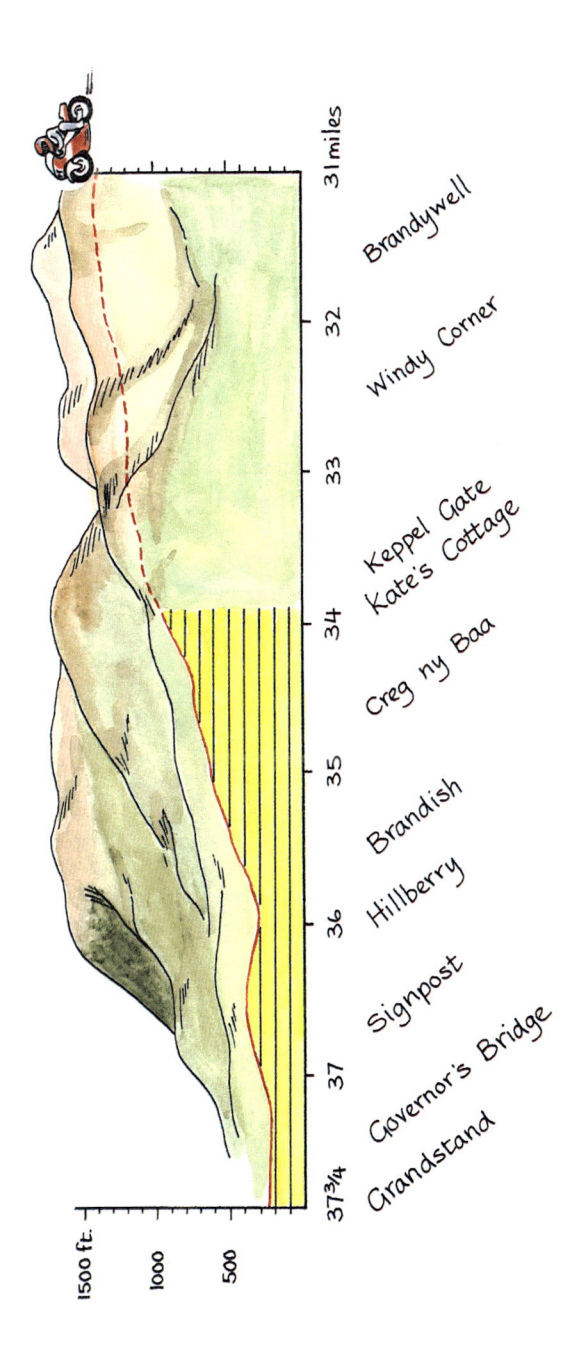

31 miles — Brandywell
32 — Windy Corner
33 — Keppel Gate
    — Kate's Cottage
34 — Creg ny Baa
35 — Brandish
36 — Hillberry
    — Signpost
37 — Governor's Bridge
37¾ — Grandstand

1500 ft.
1000
500

		Trollaby Lane. Access to internal road network. OK to park bikes. Gives access to fields adjacent to Ballahutchin Hill.
***	LTFD	**Union Mills Church.** An excellent spot. Church usually organises hospitality or you can walk back to the Post Office between races. Post Office was former home of world famous pop group The Bee Gees.
**	LT	**Union Mills Garage.** Ask permission from the proprietor.
**	FD	**Strang Road.** Access to the internal road network.
	TD	**Railway Inn.** Only a short view of the approach.
*	L	**Snugborough.** Fast stretch towards Union Mills. OK to spectate from behind the hedges of the industrial estate.
****	TFD	**Braddan Brid**ge. There are grandstands in the Church grounds and hospitality is always provided. Just before the bridge spectating is permitted from inside the course (Jubilee Oak). Here you are just 200 yards from the TT Access Road.
*		**From Quarterbridge to Braddan Bridge.** Spectating is forbidden on on the left (TT Access Road). On the right, spectators gather behind Port-e-Chee meadow wall.
****	TFD	**Quarterbridge.** A great gathering place.
*		**Devonshire Road, Alexander Drive (Woodlands), Selborne Drive, Brunswick Road.** Access from outside the course up to the rope.
****	TFD	**Bottom of Bray Hill.** Left hand side is favourite with access from Cronkbourne Road, Thorny Road, Stoney Road. The right hand side spectating positions can be reached during the race by means of the TT Access Road or by utilising the Bray Hill footbridge.
***		**Bray Hill.** Left hand side spots can be reached via Malvern Road, Hildesley Road, Lancaster Road.
**	FD	**Top of Bray Hill.** On the left St. Ninian's High School playing fields are open. On the right hand sight spectating is possible from the garage forecourt. There is a footbridge here.
**	TFD	**St. Andrews Church.** Hospitality usually provided.
*	TFD	**Nobles Park.** Close to the action. Free access with views of start and finish.
*****	TFD	**TT Grandstand.** Access at all times. Scoreboards. Full details of Race situation. Start and Finish lines. Pits.

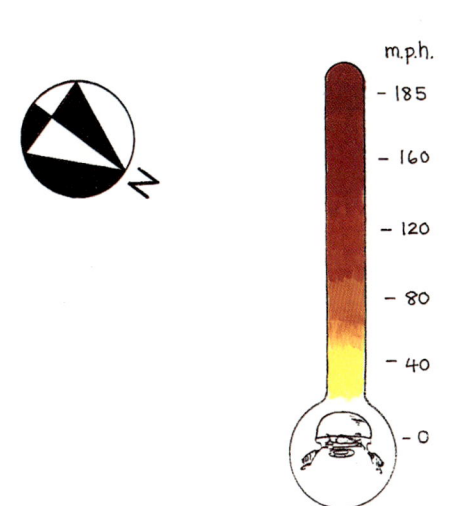

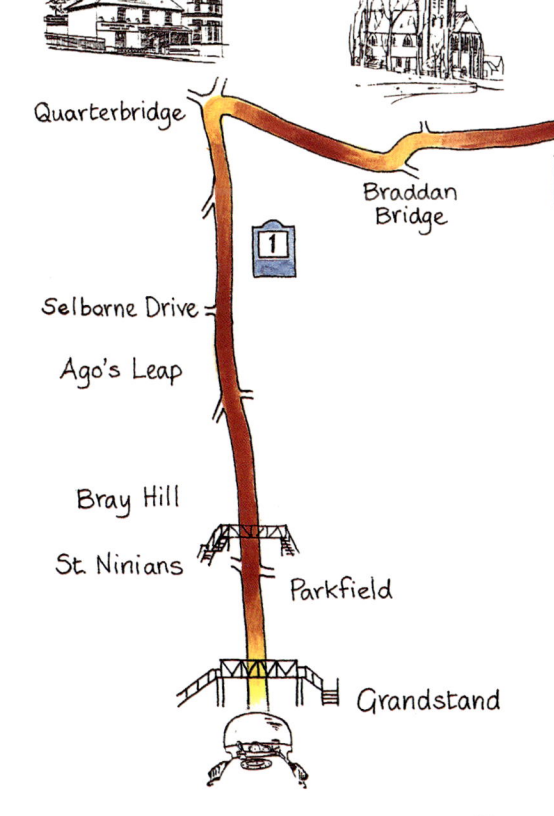

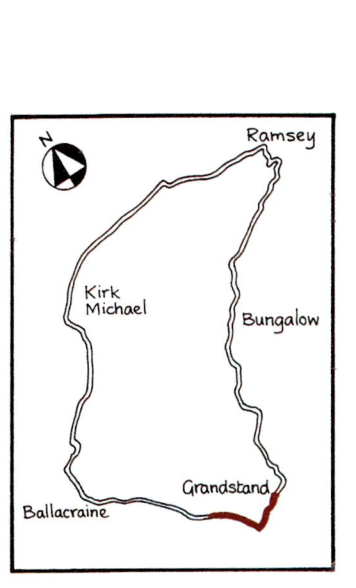

m.p.h.
- 185
- 160
- 120
- 80
- 40
- 0

TIME 1:37

N

| 3 |

Quarterbridge

Braddan Bridge

| 2 |

Snugborough

Strang Road

UNION MILLS

Trollaby Lane

| 1 |

Selbarne Drive

Ago's Leap

Bray Hill

St. Ninians

Parkfield

Grandstand

Ramsey
Kirk Michael
Bungalow
Ballacraine
Grandstand

***	LTFD	**Highlander.** One of the fastest stretches of the course. Pub now turned into a restaurant. No crossing once roads closed.
****	LTFD	**Waggon and Horses.** High speeds. Views of airborne machines. Lots of fields and hedges.
****	LTFD	**Crosby Hotel.** Plenty of parking here but you are locked in. Get here early!
*		**Crosby Crossroads.** Parking both sides of course. Pedestrians permitted to pass (on Police authority) to and from Crosby Hotel between races. Access to internal and external roads dependent on which side you park.
**	L	**Crosby Church Hall.** Access on foot only. Its height above the road makes this a good vantage point.
**	LT	**Marown Church.** About a mile of fast road in view. Cold water tap available.
		Glen Vine Road. Opposite Motor Museum. Access to the internal road network.
		Glen Darragh Road. Access to roads outside the course.
		Ballagarey Road. Access to the internal road network
		Glenlough. Farm and campsite on left hand side. Spectators must not cross here while roads are closed.

73

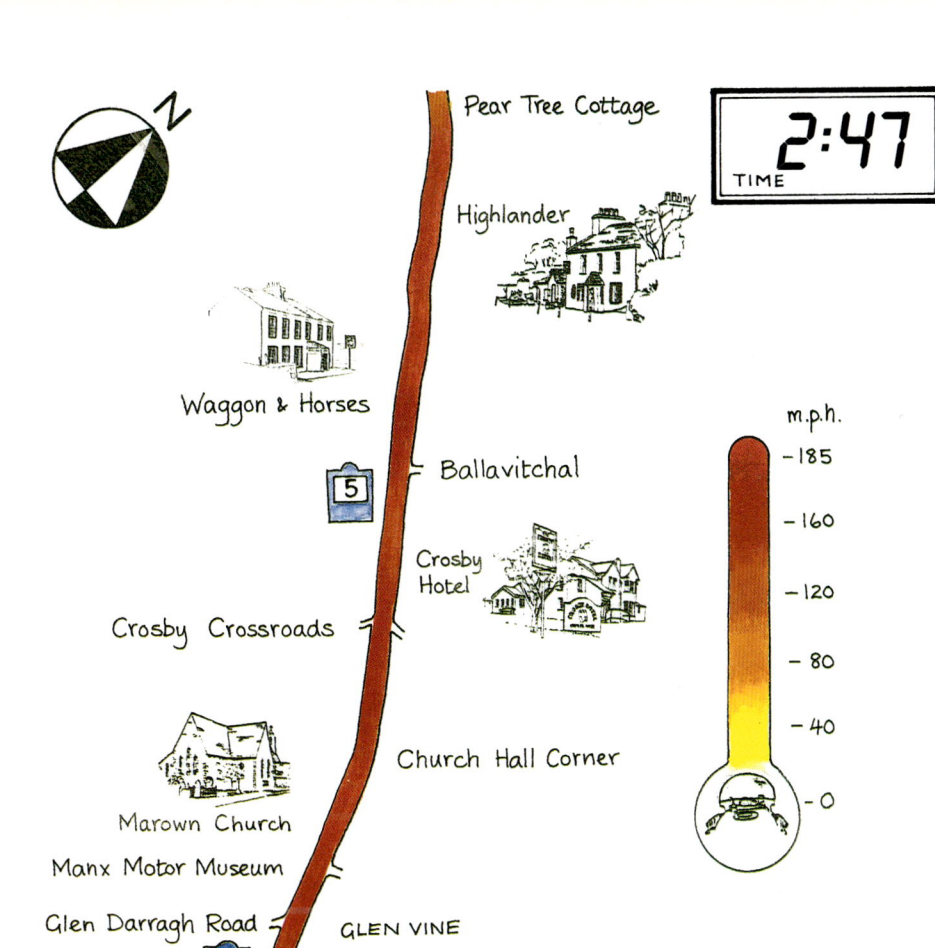

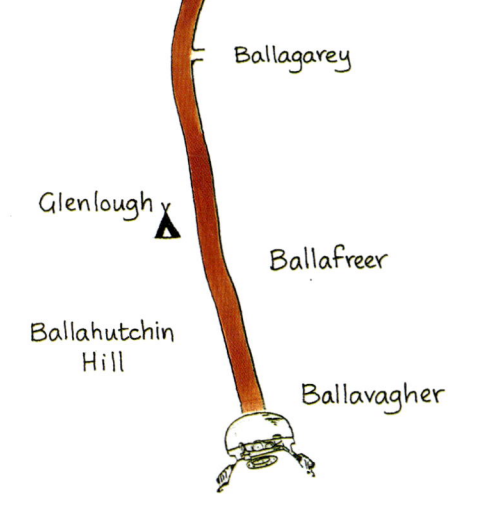

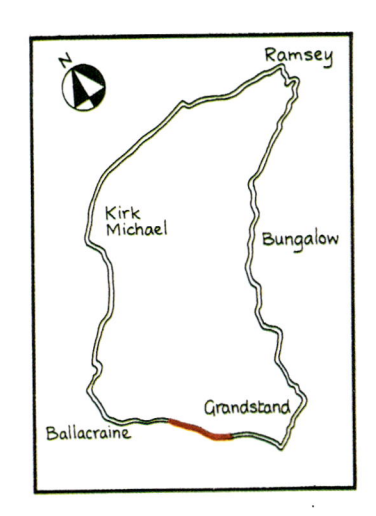

**	L	**Glen Moar Mills.** Petrol station. Limited parking.
****		**Laurel Bank.** Superb viewing here and you don't have to stay all day. Back road access from Staarvey Road – bikes only.
**		**Doran's Bend.** Named after Bill Doran, a TT regular until 1953. Bill had a spill here. The bend itself is a restricted area. Good viewing from the hillside outside the course.
**		**Ballig Bridge.** Access from the Poortown Road (A20) or on foot from Tynwald Mills to the bridge (or back towards Ballaspur).
		Ballaspur. No access.
***	TFD	**Ballacraine.** Access from the south and west. View from the south is the bend and exit. View from the west is the approach and entry. Sometimes ad hoc catering from the corner cottage. If not, all facilities from St. John's.
***	L	**Gorse Lea.** Walk back from Ballacraine.
***	L	**Ballagarraghyn.** A mile of road in view from Gorse Lea to Ballacraine. Limited parking. Open fields and hedges. By landowner's permission.
**	LTFD	**The Hawthorn.** View from Greeba Bridge to just past the pub. Ample parking. Pedestrian access to Greeba Bridge (on Police authority) between races.
***	L	**Greeba Bridge.** Reasonable parking and an excellent view of the approach to this tricky bend. Police may allow pedestrians up the road to The Hawthorn between races.
*	L	**Greeba Young Men's Hall.** Galvanised hall. Parking for several bikes with a limited view.
***	L	**Appledene.** Limited parking in country lanes. Cross road on foot before roads close. Open fields with hedges.
***	L	**Greeba Castle.** Brilliant view of this double bend if you get there early enough. Park your bike down the farm track 200 yards on left past the second bend. No cars!

m.p.h.
- 185
- 160
- 120
- 80
- 40
- 0

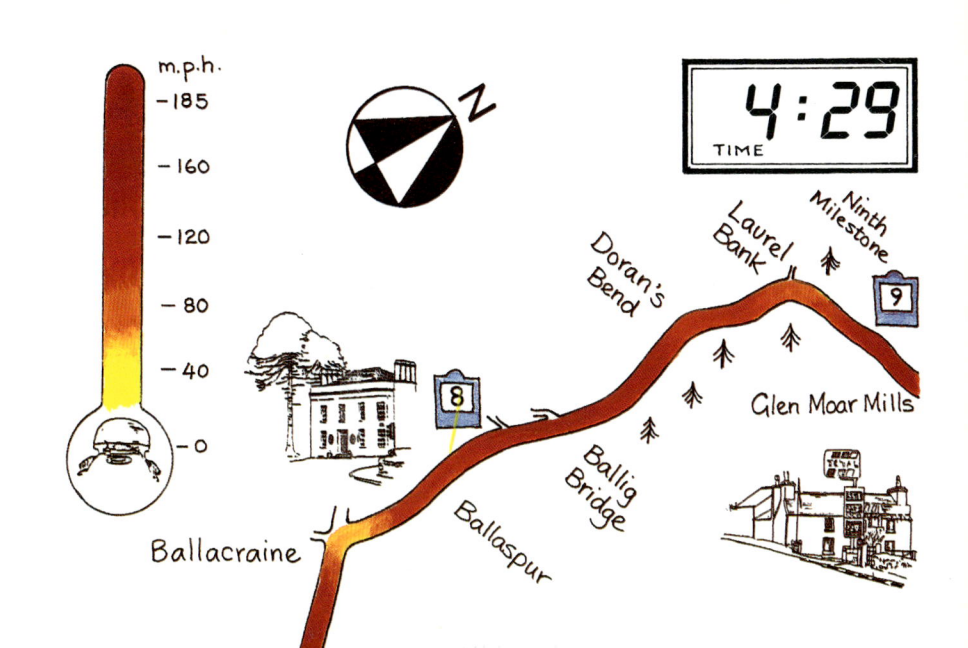

N

TIME 4:29

Ninth Milestone
Laurel Bank
Doran's Bend
9
Glen Moar Mills
Ballig Bridge
8
Ballaspur
Ballacraine
Ballagarraghyn
Gorse Lea
7
Cronk Breck
Hawthorn
Greeba Bridge
Greeba Young Mens Hall
Appledene
6
Greeba Castle

Ramsey
Kirk Michael
Bungalow
Grandstand
Ballacraine

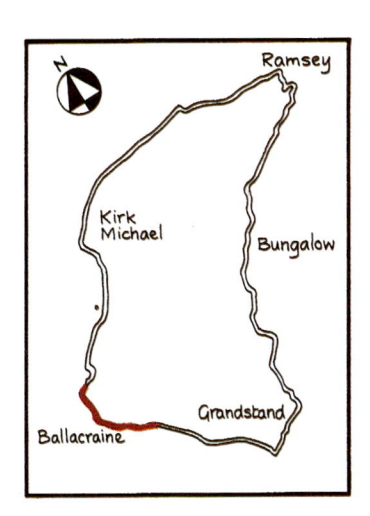

75

*	L	**Handley's Corner.** Named after Walter Handley, a famous rider who was killed in World War II. These days, there are only a few perches which can be reached on foot before the roads close. A better option is Shaughlaige Bridge, quarter of a mile before Barregarrow. Park at Barregarrow and walk back.
****	L	**Eleventh Milestone (Drinkwater's).** Drinkwater was fatally injured here in the Junior TT on 13th. June 1949. Big field inside course will hold any number of bikes and cars. Access on foot to half mile of course either side. Good view of the approach. A good day out can be had in return for a donation to the helicopter fund.
**	TFD	**Cronk-y-Voddy.** Approaching the head of the fast climb from Lambfell. Farmhouse on minor road outside the course normally offers traditional hospitality.
*	L	**Through Lambfell to Cronk-y-Voddy.** Private, mainly agricultural land both sides. Ask the farmer and observe the country code.
**		**Sarah's Cottage.** Old Sarah is long gone. Parking for a dozen cars and bikes on the left through the gateway leading up to the helipad. Usually OK to walk to Glen Helen for lunch after inspection car has toured (on Police authority).
****	LTFD	**Glen Helen.** Well organised parking with bikes in the Glen and cars on the car park. In addition to the views from the hotel grounds you can walk over the footbridge (modelled on the Menai Bridge in Anglesey) to spectate from positions back towards Black Dub. Good perches available on the bank or in the trees with views of Glen Helen and Sarah's. Hotel offers good value food and drink.
****	L	**Black Dub.** Heart stopping fast left and right with no margin for error. Small amount of parking for the enthusiast. Not for kids or the faint-hearted. Pedestrian access to Glen Helen between races normally OK (on Police authority).

77

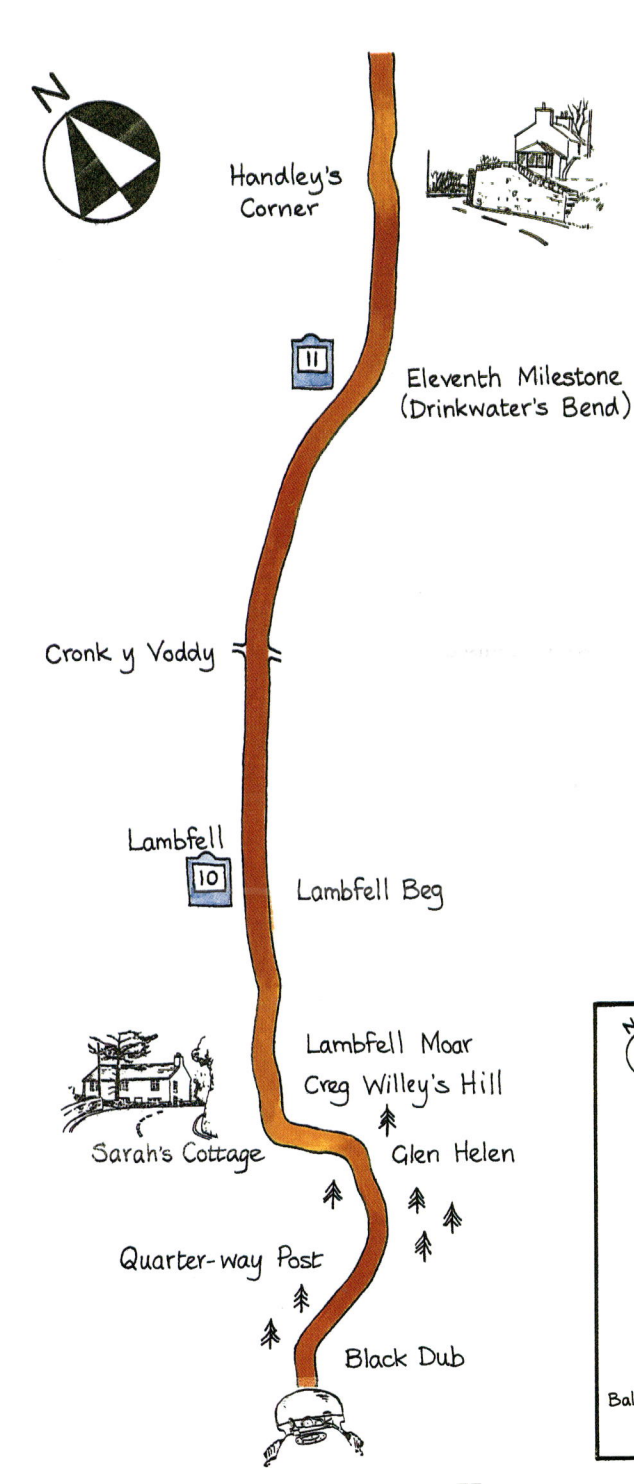

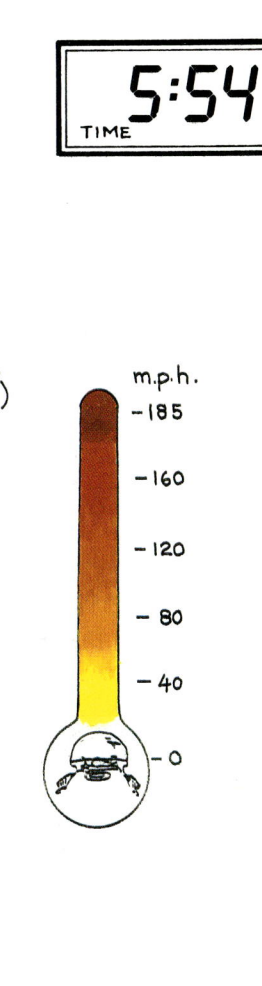

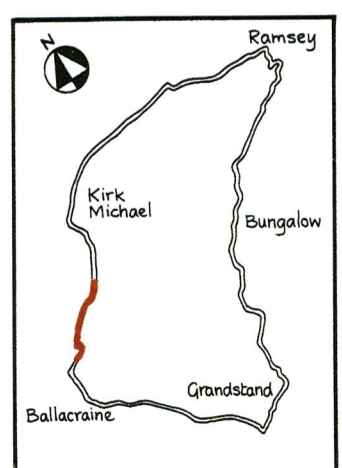

*****	L	**Rhencullen and Birkin's Bend.** Archie Birkin was killed here when he crashed whilst avoiding a fishcart during practising in 1927. From 1928 onwards roads were officially closed during practice periods. Fabulous views of the winding, rising exit from Kirk Michael. Very popular but insufficient parking. Plan ahead for a visit here. Arrive at least one hour before roads close. Pedestrian access from Orrisdale back road via old railway track.
*	L	**Kirk Michael.** Offers perches such as the Isle of Man Bank car park and the churchyard.
**	LTFD	**Mitre Hotel.** A fair view and a heightened illusion of speed as the bikes power their way through the narrow village. Good food and drink. Small garden.
***		**Douglas Road Corner.** At the junction of the A3/A4 roads. Facilities down the road in Glen Wyllin. Fast right hand approach to Kirk Michael. Normally OK to cross to the Mitre for lunch (on Police authority). If you are touring and "popping in" for a look, this is the furthest north you can approach the course from the south and west: Kirk Michael cannot be by-passed by a road vehicle from outside the course.
**	L	**Westwood.** No parking. Limited number of seats.
*	L	**Bottom of Barregarrow.** Limited parking in lane at corner.
*****		**Barregarrow.** This is the stretch where the top men gain seconds and the back markers don't. Access from inside the course B10 and outside the course via the minor road up from the A3 at the crossroads. Pedestrian access from behind the hedges from top to bottom.

N

TIME 7:20

15 Birkin's Bend

KIRK MICHAEL

Mitre Hotel

Douglas Road Corner

14 Erinville

Westwood

Cronk Urleigh

Thirteenth Milestone

13

Bottom of Barregarrow

Top of Barregarrow

Barregarrow Crossroads

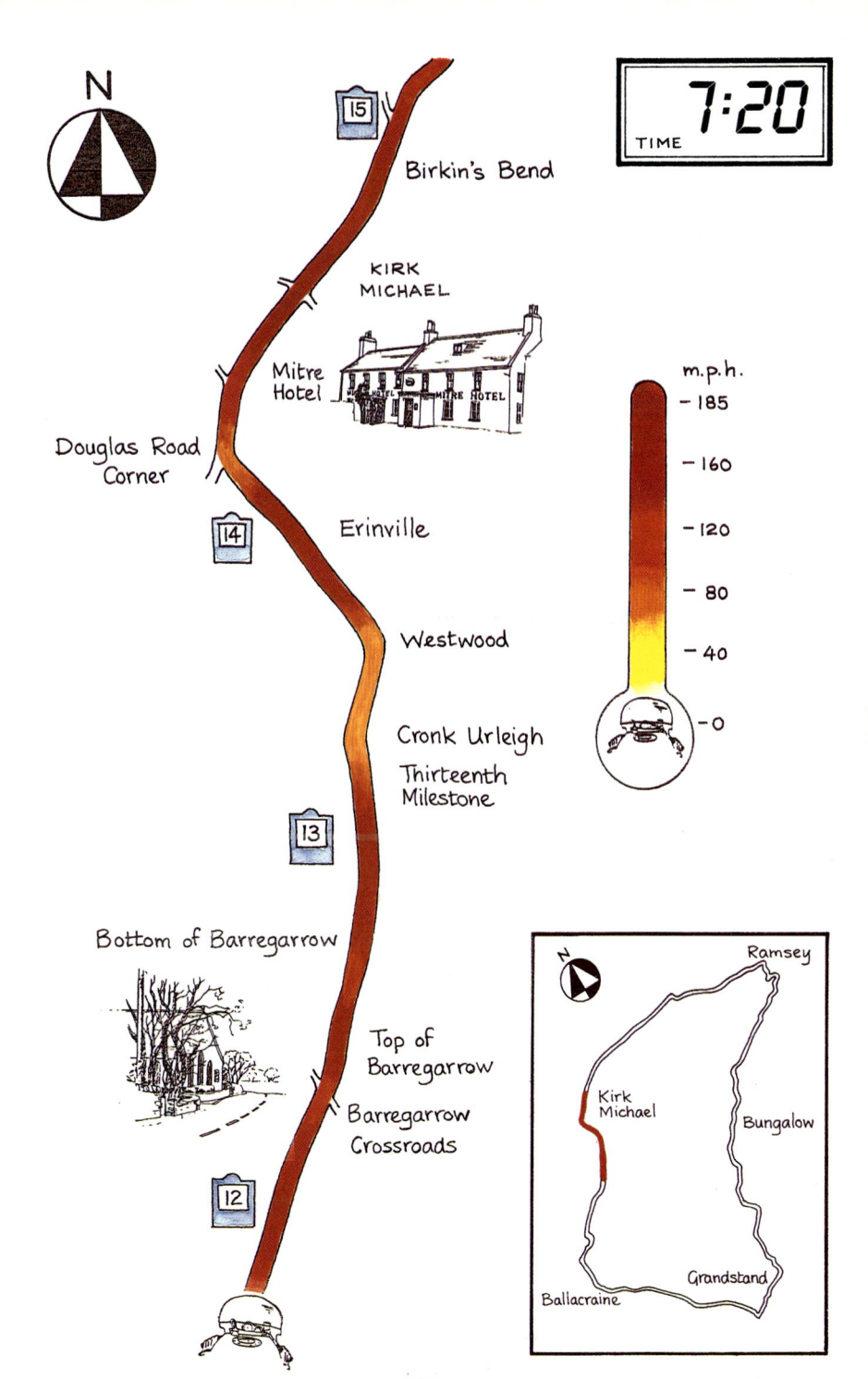

12

m.p.h.
- 185
- 160
- 120
- 80
- 40
- 0

Ramsey

Kirk Michael

Bungalow

Ballacraine

Grandstand

79

****		**Ballacrye.** This high speed leap is well worth a visit. Take the next left B9 and park 400 yards down the road then follow the track alongside the hedge in a southerly direction back to the course.
*****	TFD	**Ballaugh Bridge.** Every fan pays a visit here to watch the controlled flight from the top of the bridge to power on again on landing and a fast getaway through the village. Access from both sides A10 and Druidale Road. Police normally allow pedestrians to cross between races.
***	L	**Alpine.** Fast right hander on the approach to Ballaugh. Access for pedestrians from back road and along old railway track, approximately half mile.
**	L	**Bishopscourt.** Spectating from the Glen. Fast left-right exit.

81

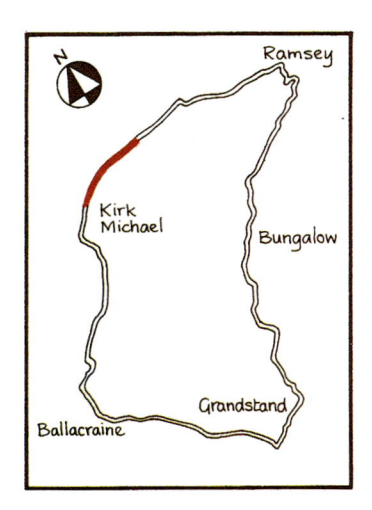

		Kerrowmoar. Spectacular riding but sadly no spectator vantage points along this stretch.
****	TFD	**Ginger Hall**. An ever popular vantage point. Good view of the power going on again after the slow Sulby Bridge corner. Access to the internal road network. Limited parking. Good hospitality.
***		**Sulby Bridge**. Plenty of parking and choice of seats on the approach – outside the course. Usually volunteers provide refreshments on busiest days.
**		**Sulby Village**. Through the village, lanes on both sides have side-tracks back to the course.
*****	TFD	**Sulby Cross Roads**. There is nowhere else in the world where you could sit in the warm early summer sunshine with a good meal and a glass on your table with only a rope between you and world class riders passing at top speed a few feet away.
*****		**Quarry Bends**. Improved roads have raised speeds through this section. Inside seats fill up early. Outside plenty of parking and viewing from Wildlife car park except restricted areas. For a quick visit there is vehicular access from the Claddaghs Road B9 and via the old railway track. Police may allow pedestrians to cross between races.

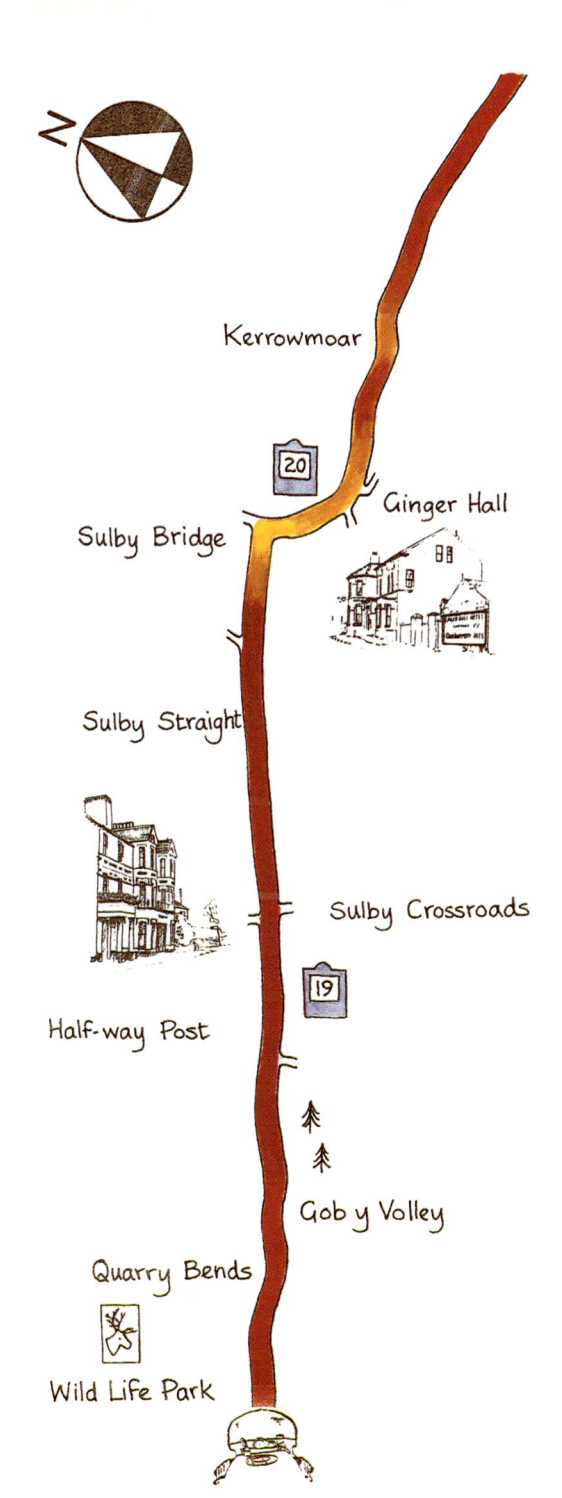

TIME 10:06

Kerrowmoar

20

Ginger Hall

Sulby Bridge

Sulby Straight

Sulby Crossroads

19

Half-way Post

Gob y Volley

Quarry Bends

Wild Life Park

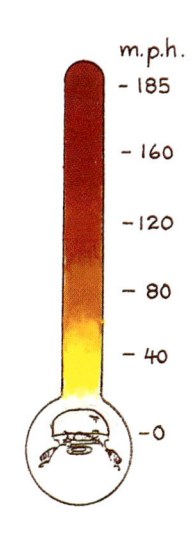

m.p.h.
- 185
- 160
- 120
- 80
- 40
- 0

Ramsey

Kirk Michael

Bungalow

Ballacraine

Grandstand

83

***	TFD	**Ramsey Bus Station.** Access via pedestrian footbridge – no loitering please.
***	TFD	**Parliament Square.** A popular vantage point. Riders brake hard for the tight right hand corner at the entrance before accelerating across the square and through the left hand bend at the exit.
**		**Schoolhouse.** A fast 90 degree left with stone walls. Spectator space on the playing fields outside the course.
****		**Milntown.** No facilities but one of the best vantage points on the course. Riders and machines become airborne over Milntown Bridge then sweep right round a right hander, shoulders tight to a stone wall on the inside. Parking OK. Arrive early for the best seats. Access via Lezayre/Greenlands housing estates.
		Milntown (Pinfold) Cottage. Prohibited area.
**	L	**Churchtown (Lezayre War Memorial).** A flat-out right-left flick between stone walls and trees. Limited parking on the Churchtown loop road.
**	L	**Glen Tramman (The Water Trough).** A dangerous 90 degree left hand corner with a difficult approach through a right hand bend which has a severe adverse camber. Limited spectator accommodation. Arrive early for a good seat!
***	L	**Glen Duff.** A flat out, virtually straight stretch of road with a bumpy approach through a slight right hand bend where the machines become airborne. Limited space for the connoisseur. Can be reached from the Bayr-ny-Hayrey Road B14 via the Ramsey – St. Judes A13.

TIME 11:27

Parliament Square
Ramsey Bus Station
Raymotors
School House Corner

N

m.p.h.
- 185
- 160
- 120
- 80
- 40
- 0

23

Pinfold Cottage
Milntown

Ballakillingan
22

Glentramman

21 Glenduff

Ramsey
Kirk Michael
Bungalow
Ballacraine
Grandstand

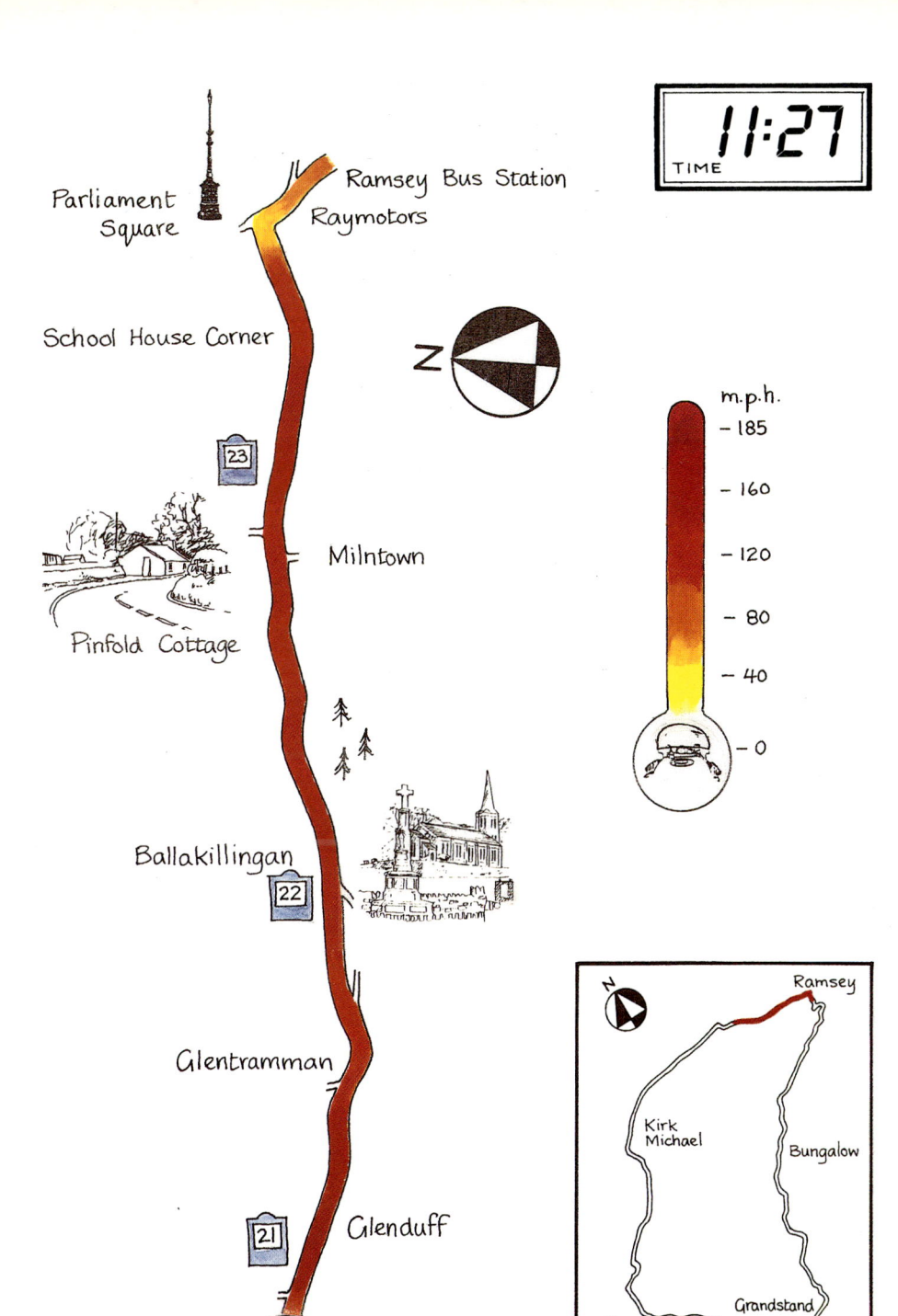

85

***		**Guthrie's**. Parking strictly limited between the Gooseneck and the Bungalow. One of the most enjoyable experiences is to park at one of these spots well before the road closes then hike to a mid-point. Re-trace your steps during the race to enjoy dozens of different views.
***	T	**Gooseneck**. Access and parking via Hibernian back road junction of A2/A15. A tight rising right hander.
***		**Hairpin to Gooseneck.** Inside, the paths and tracks on Lhergy Frissel give access to several perches. Outside, the land falls away steeply giving some difficult but interesting worm's eye views.
Note		**Hairpin to Hillberry**. There are very few restricted areas on either side of the course. The land is a mixture of government and privately owned; nearly all of which is given over to sheep grazing. Please observe the country code at all times.
****		**Ramsey Hairpin**. A tight, rising hairpin corner with a natural grandstand on the inside of the course. Can be reached via Claughbane Walk during road closed periods. Park carefully on this ambulance access road.
***		**Stella Maris. Private House**. A rising right hand bend where riders "scratch" short circuit style. No parking here but well worth the walk from the Hairpin or Ballure. Viewing from the elevated private garden for a contribution to the Red Cross.
***		**Whitegate**. Difficult left hand bend with bumpy approach and adverse camber. Parking outside the course but limited spectator accommodation. The exit, past the entrance to Barrule Park is a prohibited area.
*****		**Cruickshanks (May Hill)**. All facilities a short distance away in Ramsey. A sweeping right hander with a short straight approach. Extremely bumpy, testing rider and machine to the limit. It is an awesome sight to watch top riders hurtling between the telegraph poles, stone walls and kerbs.

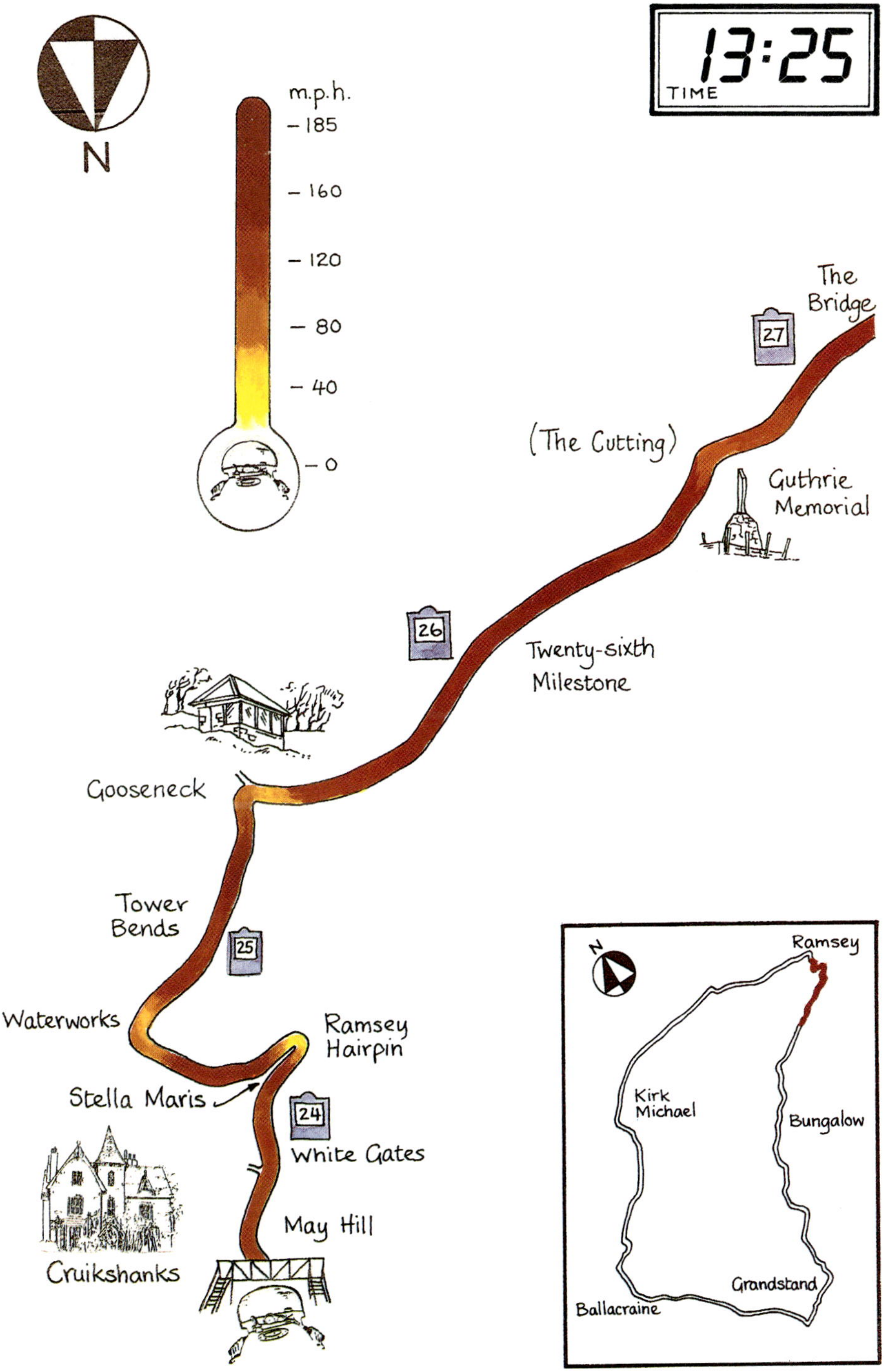

N
m.p.h.
185
160
120
80
40
0
13:25
TIME
The Bridge
27
(The Cutting)
Guthrie Memorial
26
Twenty-sixth Milestone
Gooseneck
Tower Bends
25
Waterworks
Ramsey Hairpin
Stella Maris
24
White Gates
May Hill
Cruikshanks
N
Ramsey
Kirk Michael
Bungalow
Grandstand
Ballacraine

****   **Verandah.** Although access is permitted outside the course for most of the way you are well below the road level and out of sight of the bikes. It is possible, with care – for bikes only – to get to the old Snaefell mine workings via Agneash village and from there walk up to this section. Inside the course offers exciting viewing.

***   **Black Hut.** Sited in an old quarry this shelter is on a fast left hand bend leading the machines onto the Verandah section.

***   **George's Folly.** One of the newer names on the course, named after Alex George on the occasion of his spill when in second place on the last lap of the 1977 Senior. Fast right hander.

***   **Mountain Box.** Sometimes known as the East Mountain Gate. Located on a sharp and unforgiving left hander.

***   **Mountain Mile.** Fast and clear section of the mountain affording riders clear views of any other competitors in the near vicinity.

14:50 TIME

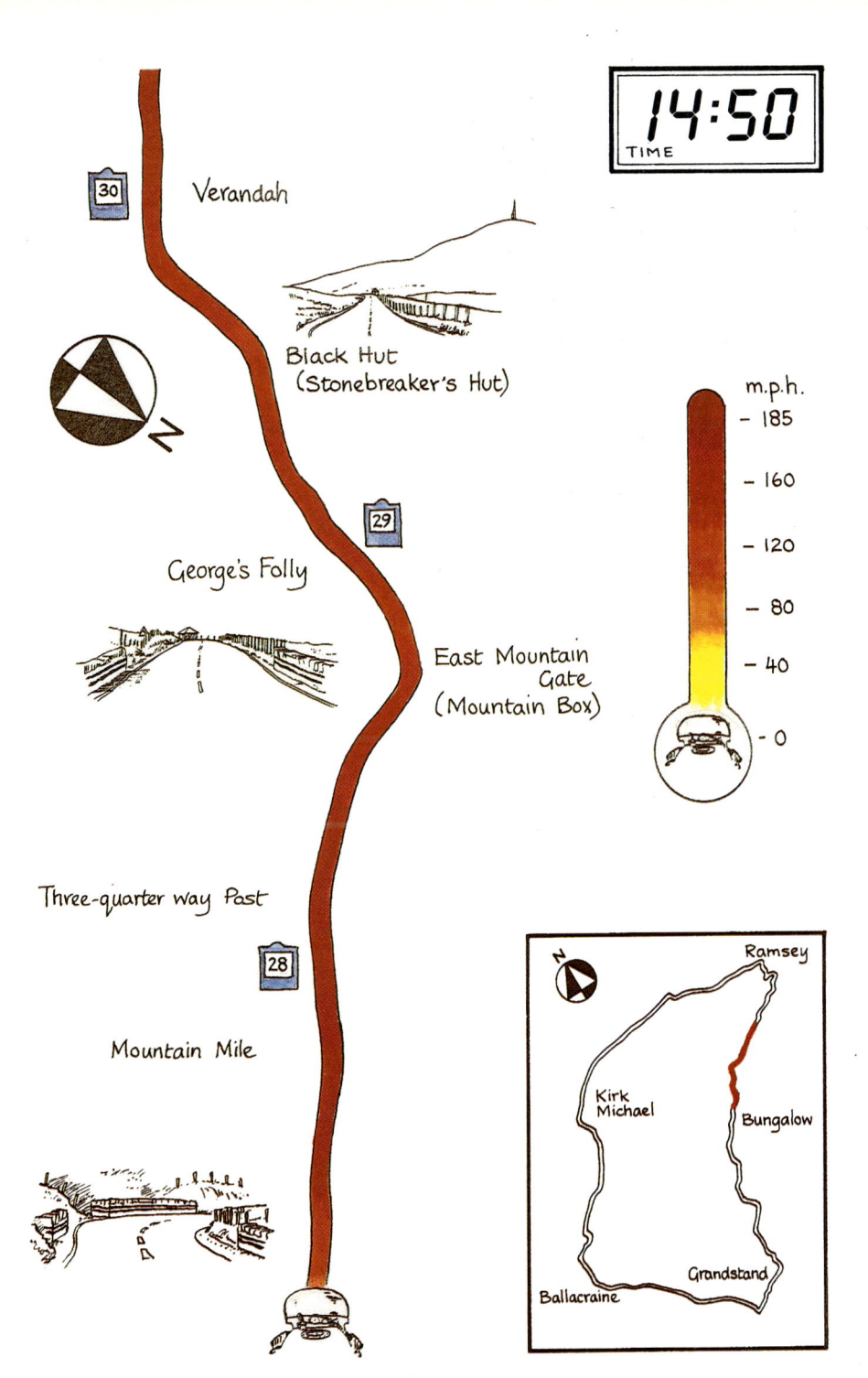

Verandah

Black Hut
(Stonebreaker's Hut)

m.p.h.
- 185
- 160
- 120
- 80
- 40
- 0

George's Folly

East Mountain
Gate
(Mountain Box)

Three-quarter way Past

Mountain Mile

Ramsey
Kirk Michael
Bungalow
Ballacraine
Grandstand

89

***		**Thirty Third Milestone.** Approximately half-way between Windy Corner and Keppel Gate this section is best viewed from the high ground outside the course. Tough left handers. Parking at Windy Corner or the old Quarry workings a quarter of mile beyond. Need to be early for best position.
****		**Windy Corner.** A fair amount of parking here provided you are early enough. Skill required in varying conditions to master this right hander. Listen to weather forecast before heading into the mountains. It is possible with care to bike down a Mountain track into Glen Roy and then on into Laxey or the back roads to Creg-ny-Baa or Onchan.
***		**Thirty Second Milestone.** Three excellent fast left handers. Good spectating from the high banks on the outside of the course. Prohibited on inside. Park at Windy Corner and walk.
****		**Brandywell.** Good parking on this fast left hander. Worth a visit to observe riding styles. Easy access for spectating all the way back to the Bungalow on both sides of the course. The B10 allows freedom of movement to all parts of the internal road network.
***		**Hailwood Rise.** Accelerating hard up the hill from the Bungalow there are fine views to be had on both sides of the road. From here on it's downhill almost all the way home.
*****	TFD	**Bungalow.** Always lots of activity here with parking for hundreds of bikes and cars. Competitors are in sight – in good weather – from when they exit the Verandah all the way to Brandywell. Access during racing by the Snaefell Mountain Railway. Change of venue possible by using A14 to Sulby Straight or Ginger Hall. Well used footbridge here but please do not linger or take flash photographs.
****		**Bungalow Bridge (Les Graham Memorial).** A super spot to walk to from the Bungalow across the front of the well-worth-a-visit Murray's Motor Museum. Very fast left hander with three-quarters of a mile of road in view.

Thirty-third Milestone

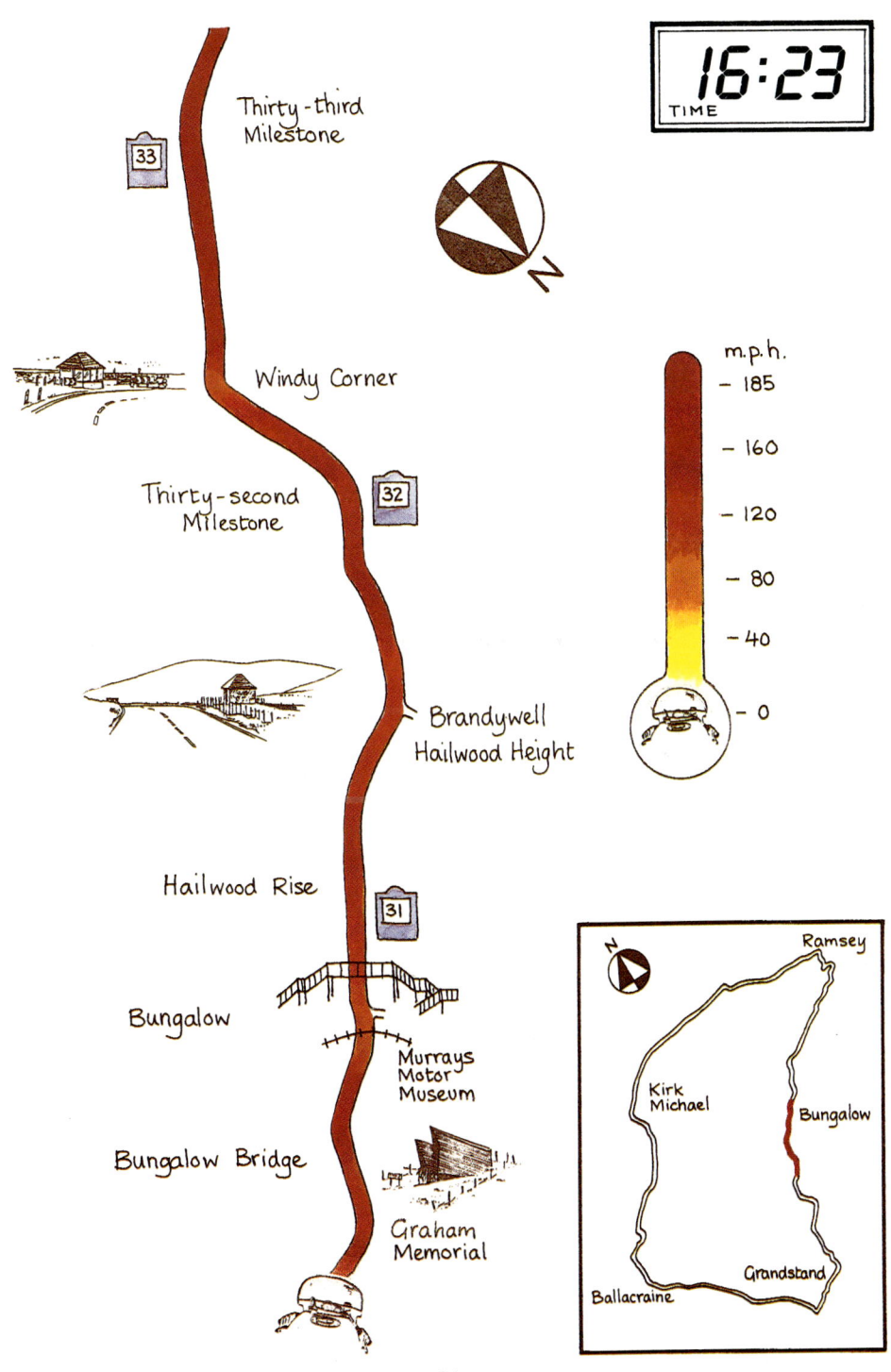

33

Windy Corner

Thirty-second Milestone

32

Brandywell Hailwood Height

Hailwood Rise

31

Bungalow

Murrays Motor Museum

Bungalow Bridge

Graham Memorial

TIME 16:23

m.p.h.
- 185
- 160
- 120
- 80
- 40
- 0

Ramsey
Kirk Michael
Bungalow
Ballacraine
Grandstand

91

***		**Cronk-ny-Mona.** Spectating possible here from campsite entrance right up to road junction. Very thrilling part of course. Access to internal road network and via Willaston footbridge to TT Grandstand area. In the right place you can pick up first signs of approaching riders as far away as Kate's.
*****	TD	**Hillberry.** Superb view of the final descent from the mountain and a stylish fast right hand exit. The fields are private and boggy. Best place is the small grandstand which holds around 200 people. Access via Little Mill back road from Onchan.
****	LT	**Brandish.** A fast left hand corner before the scorch down to Hillberry. Some parking in the inside field but you need to be there well before roads close. Named after Walter Brandish who broke a leg here in 1923 which ended his racing career.
*****	L	**Gob-ny-Geay** . No facilities but an excellent position to spectate from on top of the highest hedges on the course. Glimpses back to Kate's and road in view from Creg-ny-Baa to Brandish. The meaning of Gob-ny-Geay is "the mouth or beak of the wind".
*****	TFD	**Creg-ny-Baa.** Possibly the premier spectating spot outside of Douglas. All facilities, plenty of parking, access by coach. Pay to use grandstands or ramble for a perch in the heather. Lots of road in view from Kate's to beyond Gob-ny-Geay. Good hospitality.
****		**Kate's Cottage to Creg-ny-Baa.** Park at the Creg then trek up the moorland behind the hedges on the outside of the course for different views of this magnificent downhill plunge. Do not attempt to cross after the roads are closed. P.S. There never was a Kate: it was slip of the tongue by Graham Walker (Murray's Dad) during a pre-war BBC commentary . . . the occupants, the Tate family didn't seem to mind and the name lives on!
****	L	**Keppel Gate.** Good view of the Thirty Third and the fast approach to Keppel. TT luxury is to arrive early by car, park in a grandstand position and enjoy the racing, commentary and the atmosphere without worrying about the weather. Spectating possible on both sides of the road.

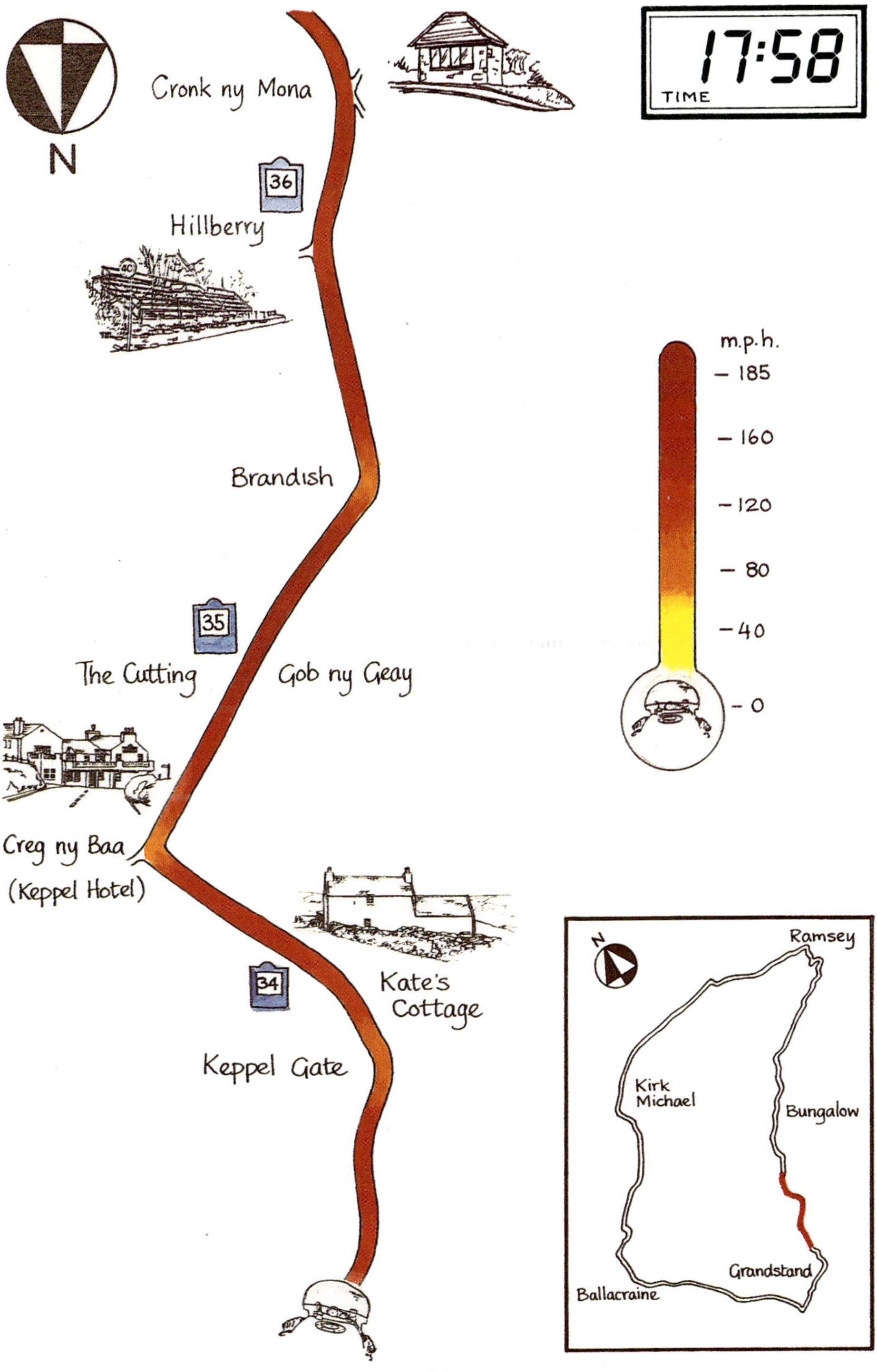
17:58
TIME
N
Cronk ny Mona
36
Hillberry
40
Brandish
m.p.h.
185
160
120
80
40
0
35
The Cutting
Gob ny Geay
Creg ny Baa
(Keppel Hotel)
34
Kate's Cottage
Keppel Gate
N
Ramsey
Kirk Michael
Bungalow
Grandstand
Ballacraine

*****   TFD   **TT Grandstand.** Always an exciting place to spectate even during practising. Watch the young scouts in action on the scoreboards, the timekeepers, the painters transposing times onto the lap boards – it might be old style – but it's part of the TT magic. Scrutineers at work in the pits. The furious activities of the mechanics and support teams. Peter Kneale's lucid commentaries, Geoff Cannell's famous sprints up and down the pit lane bringing the latest news via Manx Radio...oh and you might just notice the bikes flashing past at some incredible speed!

An early visit to the Grandstand area helps in appreciating the sheer size of the Meeting. With an open choice of seating arrangements it has long been a favourite for the press and offers excellent photographic opportunities. There is also the chance that you can meet and talk to the riders. Visit the winners enclosure and see the TT stars. Browse amongst the many stalls at the back of the Grandstand.

**   **Governor's Bridge.** Tightest and slowest bend on the course and a great favourite with photographers. Wide choice of spectating positions both inside and outside of course.

The Nook. Restricted area.

***   **Bedstead.** Watch the chase down towards Governor's from inside the housing estates. Access from Watterson Lane on the inside, from Onchan on the outside. The old iron bedstead is long gone but the more recent railings do have an interesting design.

****   **Signpost Corner.** A terrific spot. Altered over the years and producing high speed cornering it still retains its magnetism for the fans. All eyes at the Grandstand are fixed on the "rider past Signpost light" on the scoreboards and all ears are tuned into the commentary for the magic words "the lights on now – he's through Signpost". Plenty of parking down the slip road, accessed from Onchan. A good place to watch the closing stages of the Race.

19:00 TIME

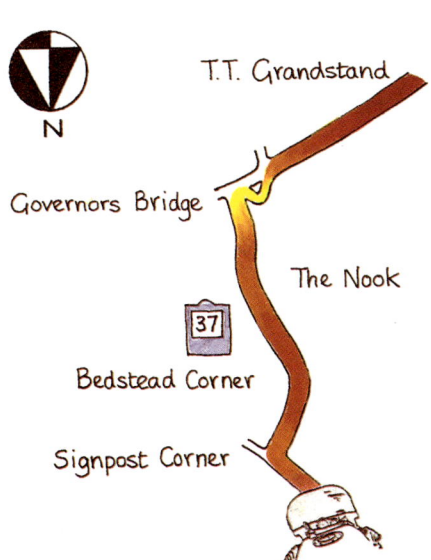

T.T. Grandstand

Governors Bridge

The Nook

37

Bedstead Corner

Signpost Corner

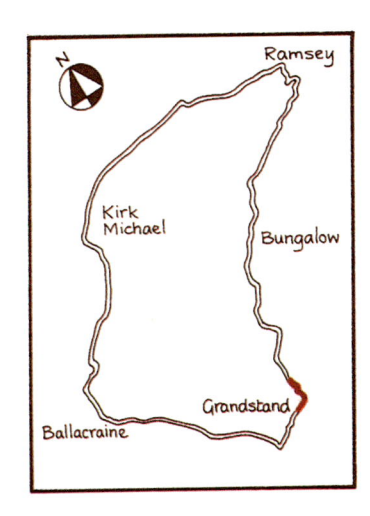

Ramsey

Kirk Michael

Bungalow

Ballacraine

Grandstand

Crossleys

CERTIFIED ACCOUNTANTS & REGISTERED AUDITORS

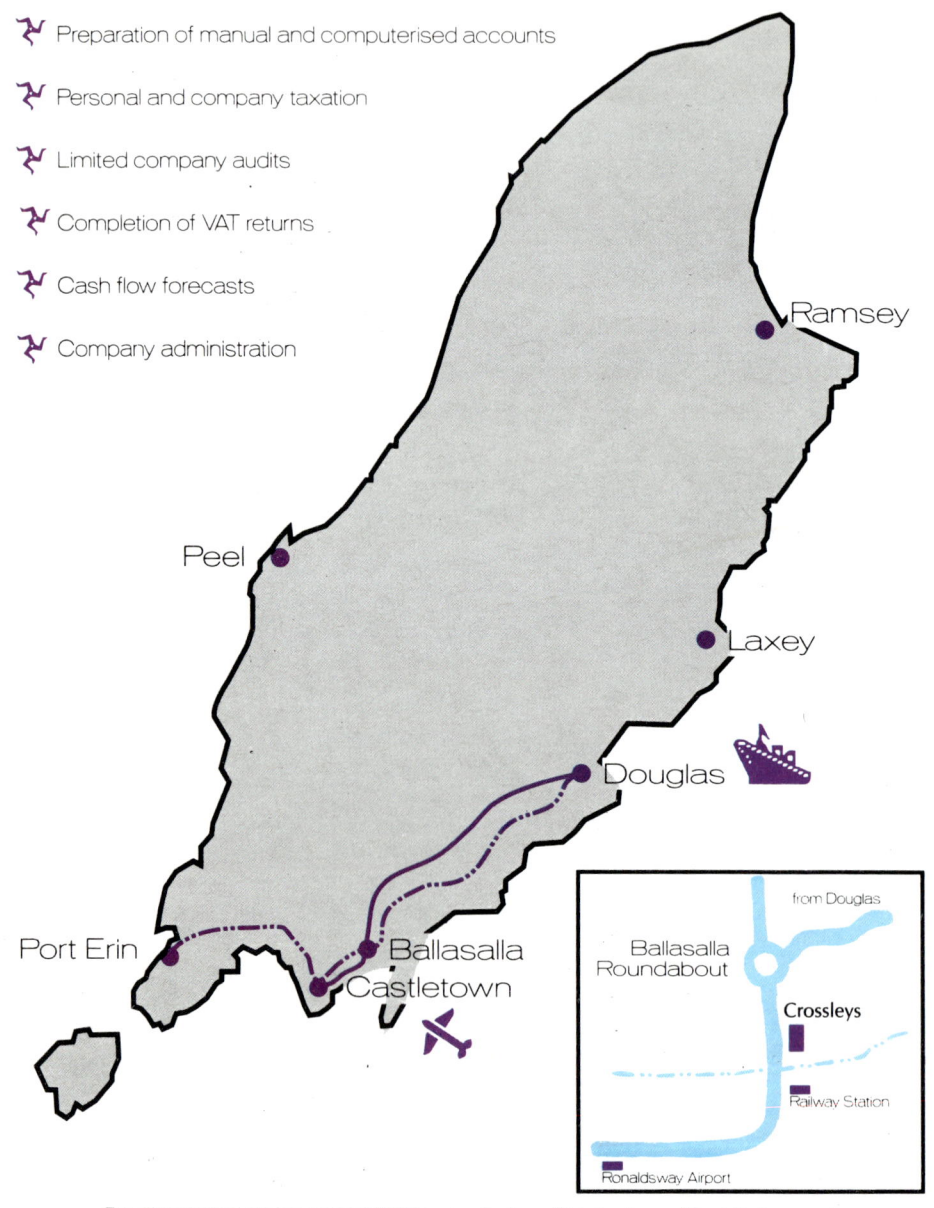

- Preparation of manual and computerised accounts
- Personal and company taxation
- Limited company audits
- Completion of VAT returns
- Cash flow forecasts
- Company administration

For all enquiries please contact Bill Harvey, Andrew Pennington or Nigel Rotheroe at:
Crossleys, P.O. Box 1, Portland House, Station Road, Ballasalla, Isle of Man
Telephone 0624 822816 Facsimile 0624 824570